# Real Lives, Eternal Lessons

## Learning from Women of the New Testament

N. A. ROGERS

Also by

N. A. ROGERS

A Bible Study Focused on Fasting

Eunuchs, A Bible Study

https://abiblestudyon.com

ISBN: 979-8-9949289-0-5 (sc)
ISBN: 979-8-9949289-1-2 (e)

# Dedication

It has been twenty years since my mother passed, yet her wisdom continues to guide me. I often reflect on her words and wish I had been a more attentive student while she was still here.

This work is dedicated to mothers—the women who shaped us, corrected us, encouraged us, and taught us to become better people. Scripture preserves the lives and faith of many women and mothers so that we, too, may continue to learn from them, generation to generation.

# *Introduction*

The purpose of this study is to highlight the actions of women in Scripture so we can imitate their godly examples, learn from their missteps, and in all things glorify God. Throughout the Bible, the Lord gives us living portraits of faith, courage, and surrender, as well as examples about actions to avoid. Just as women learn from Abraham, Joseph, and Daniel, men can learn from Elizabeth, Mary, Priscilla, and even Herodias. Studying the women of the Bible deepens our understanding and reminds us that every biblical character contributes to the whole counsel of God.

As we spend time with these individuals, we step into their stories and discover how human struggles and responses remain strikingly similar across the centuries. Cultures change, but the heart of our challenges does not. At the end of this study, you'll find reasons to remember their story. Wrestling with faith? Consider Mary, Anna, or Martha. Battling pride? Reflect on Herodias, Sapphira, or the Canaanite woman. Let's allow these Biblical examples to lead us in glorifying God, the best lessons often come from real lives.

This study includes over 60 women and groups mentioned in the New Testament. Thirty-three are named, including six different Marys, while others are identified by role or circumstance. There are groups of widows, prominent women, and women in prison. Notably, the majority of the women, about 64%, are widows or mentioned without husbands. For example: Mary and Martha, Phoebe, Lydia, weeping sinner, Mary Magdalene, and Tabitha may have been married, but no spouses are mentioned. While some spouses are implied or named, only a few couples appear in the New Testament: Elizabeth and Zechariah, Mary and Joseph, Priscilla and Aquilla, Herodias and Antipas, Annanias and Sapphira, Felix and Drusilla, Pilot and his wife.

Begin each section by reading the narrative retelling that centers on the woman (or women) in each passage, then the full Biblical account. Frequently the women in the passage may play a lessor role or be overlooked, but the narrative tries to focus on the women in the scripture. Let us learn from these first-century women and the events where they participated; whose actions still instruct and inspire. For those who enjoy historical context, an appendix provides general background on first-century governments and leaders.

Additional material on this topic and teaching material should be available at: **https://abiblestudyon.com**

# *Acknowledgements*

Each time I study the Bible, I encounter new insights and perspectives that deepen my understanding and reveal areas where my earlier interpretations were incomplete. Any errors that remain are unintentional and are entirely my own.

I am sincerely grateful for the encouragement of Rick and April, the thoughtful input of Karen and Lynn, and the shared study, prayer, and fellowship with Sara, Genny, Shana, Donna, Brenda, Kim, and Torri.

# *Table of Contents*

# *Elizabeth*

*Luke 1:5-80*

Fifteen to eighteen months before the birth of Jesus, a woman named Elizabeth lived quietly in the hill country of Judah, a rugged region nestled between Jerusalem and Hebron. According to tradition, her home was located about five miles west of Jerusalem, roughly a two-hour walk over rocky hills.

Elizabeth was no ordinary woman. She was a daughter of Aaron, born into the priestly line. A heritage that would have made her a highly desirable bride (Ilan, 1996, p. 59). The tribe of Levi served at the temple, but only sons of Aaron were priests. With high prospects, she married Zechariah, also from Aaron's lineage and an active priest. Zechariah would have served in one of the twenty-four divisions that took turns ministering in the Temple at Jerusalem (each division served for one week, twice a year, along with the major festivals). They would have been an honored and respected couple, knowledgeable of the law and traditions.

Together, Elizabeth and Zechariah were known for their righteousness and devotion, faithfully observing all of God's commandments. But they had no children. In their culture, childlessness carried social and spiritual implications. Children were considered both a sign of divine favor and a source of security in old age. Elizabeth and Zechariah were both from priestly families and would have had high expectations to add to Aaron's lineage with children. According to rabbinic legal expectation, if a couple remained childless after ten years, the man was permitted, even expected, to take another wife (Mishnah Yevamot 6:6; Ilan, 1996, 106). He was expected to 'be fruitful and multiply'. But Zechariah did not divorce his wife. His loyalty to Elizabeth, even amid societal pressure and personal disappointment, speaks to their close relationship and faithfulness.

While Zechariah was away in Jerusalem serving his rotation in the Temple, something extraordinary happened. As he ministered at the altar of incense, Gabriel, the angel of the Lord, appeared beside him. Zechariah was gripped with fear.

*"Do not be afraid, Zechariah, for your prayer has been heard, and your wife Elizabeth will bear you a son, and you shall name him John. "You will have joy and gladness, and many will rejoice over his birth. "For he will be great in the sight of the Lord; and he will drink no wine or liquor, and he will be filled with the Holy Spirit while still in his mother's womb. "And he will turn many of the sons of Israel back to the Lord their God. "And it is he who will go as a forerunner before Him in the spirit and power of Elijah, TO TURN THE HEARTS OF FATHERS BACK TO THEIR CHILDREN, and the disobedient to the attitude of the righteous, to make ready a people prepared for the Lord." Luke 1:13b-17*

A prophecy that his son would be a prophet like Elijah! He would turn the hearts of the fathers to their children. It had been almost 400 years since the last prophet, Malachi, spoke.

*"Behold, I am going to send you Elijah the prophet before the coming of the great and terrible day of the LORD. He will turn the hearts of the fathers back to their children and the hearts of the children to their fathers, so that I will not come and strike the land with complete destruction." Malachi 4:5-6*

Zechariah, like many of us might have, hesitated in belief, and as a result, he was struck mute, unable to speak. Yet those waiting outside the temple for his morning blessing sensed that something remarkable had happened. It would have been a silent but extraordinary blessing.

When his time of priestly service ended, Zechariah returned home. Although girls were not included in formal schools, the wealthy may have hired tutors for daughters, or they may have been homeschooled in reading and writing. Zechariah evidently found a way to communicate the angel Gabriel's message to Elizabeth, though scripture does not record how this occurred. (Ilan, 1996, pages 190 -192, 204). They would have a son who would be a prophet! It must have been a quiet but exciting time in their home!

Soon, Elizabeth conceived. For five months, she kept her news to herself. Perhaps, as an older woman, she feared there might be a miscarriage, whether due to age, menopause, or uncertainty about the physical signs. She may have waited to be sure before telling others. Still, her heart rejoiced, as she declared,

> *"Thus the Lord has done for me in the days when he looked on me, to take away my reproach among people." (Luke 1:25).*

Elizabeth expresses the failure she felt to not have children and recognizes God's hand in her pregnancy. People could no longer look down on her for her barrenness. She was going to have a son! Not only a child, but a prophet! Their son would become the man Malachi prophesied about. Can you imagine the joy and pride she felt at being part of Jehovah's plan? Elizabeth would no longer feel the reproach of being childless. She and Zechariah were chosen by Jehovah to have a son.

When Elizabeth was in her sixth month, the angel Gabriel appeared again, this time to a young woman in Nazareth named Mary, engaged but not yet married. Gabriel told her she would conceive by the Holy Spirit and bear a miraculous child, the Son of the Most High. As a sign, Gabriel mentioned her relative's, Elizabeth, unexpected pregnancy.

Mary responded with faith and quickly made the long journey, over 70 miles on foot, likely taking 3 to 5 days to the hill country of Judah. When Mary entered the house and greeted Elizabeth, the baby in Elizabeth's womb leapt with joy. In that moment, Elizabeth was filled with the Holy Spirit and began to prophesy:

> *"Blessed are you among women and blessed is the fruit of your womb! And how has it happened to me that the mother of my Lord would come to me? For behold, when*

*the sound of your greeting reached my ears, the baby leaped in my womb for joy. And blessed is she who believed that there would be a fulfillment of what had been spoken to her by the Lord." Luke 1:42b-45.*

Elizabeth, not Peter, not John the Baptist, and not even Zechariah, first proclaimed the arrival of the Messiah! Her words must have been an incredible reassurance to Mary, a young, unmarried teen who had just received the astonishing news that she would bear the Messiah.

Elizabeth, who was probably adjusting to her new role as future mother to John the prophet, meets the future mother of the Messiah! Elizabeth's and John's role would be secondary and supportive of the Messiah. Some from a priestly home might feel jealous or disappointed that their position was subordinate, but Elizabeth greeted and opened her heart to Mary with joy and humility.

Later, John the Baptist mimics his mom's attitude. In John 3:22-26, John the Baptist's followers complain that more disciples are going to Jesus. John's response in verses 27-33 explain that he must decrease as the Messiah will increase. He, like his mother, understood his role for the Messiah and expressed joy at His coming.

How valuable for Mary to spend time with a righteous, older woman who was also experiencing a miraculous pregnancy, though under very different circumstances. Mary stayed with Elizabeth for about three months, likely remaining through the birth of John.

During the last trimester of Elizabeth's pregnancy, Mary would have helped and watched closely. She also provided someone for Elizabeth to talk with! Elizabeth, for her part, knew Mary's situation: unmarried, engaged (betrothed), pregnant, and yet carrying the Lord. When Mary shared her story, she knew Elizabeth believed her, even if others might not. Elizabeth had blessed her, prophesied over her, and affirmed all that Gabriel had said. Elizabeth offered Mary the spiritual and emotional support she would likely not receive from others in Nazareth once she returned home.

On the eighth day after John's birth, friends and family gathered for the circumcision ceremony. Everyone assumed the child would be named after his father, Zechariah. But Elizabeth declared that his name would be John, a name meaning *"The Lord is gracious."* They ignored Elizabeth, turning to Zechariah for his decision. Still mute, he took a tablet and wrote, "His name is John." Instantly, his speech was restored, and he began to praise God.

A sense of awe and reverence fell upon all who witnessed it. The people recognized that the hand of the Lord was with this child and began to ask, *"What then will this child become?"* After 400 years without a prophet in Israel, this moment should have stirred widespread expectation, but life moves on, and thirty years later, people forget.

Elizabeth and Zechariah, both righteous and faithful, understood the significance. They knew that John would be a prophet of the Most High, destined to prepare the way for the Lord (Luke 1:76). As elderly parents, they likely did not live to see his ministry unfold or feel the pain of his death. Scripture tells us that John remained in the wilderness until the time came for his public appearance in Israel (Luke 1:80).

Elizabeth's story is found only in the Gospel of Luke. Luke highlights several key women during the life and ministry of Jesus. Luke, a companion of the apostle Paul and probably a Gentile, wrote both the Gospel of Luke and the book of Acts which records the early spread of the Gospel. Most scholars believe Luke's Gospel was written after Mark and Matthew, likely between 70 and 80 CE after the destruction of the Temple. Luke provides additional information and a different perspective, sharing Elizabeth's story.

## *Reflection on Elizabeth*

In spending time with individuals included in the Bible, we put ourselves in their position. What would we have done? How did they keep their faith? How did God help them? These questions are to help us see the events from their perspective.

1. As a daughter of the sons of Aaron, Elizabeth would have been a highly regarded bride. But she describes herself as having *'reproach'* for her childlessness. Have you ever felt dejected in how others see you because of unmet expectations or delayed hopes? How could Elizabeth's story help you?

2. Elizabeth went from feeling disgraced to having a miraculous pregnancy. Her son would be a prophet like Elijah! You can feel her joy.... Then, a teen girl comes who has an even more miraculous pregnancy. What was Elizabeth's response to Mary's news that her son would be the Messiah? What were some reactions we might have when other's news overshadows us?

3. Based on her actions and those around her, what are Elizabeth's strengths?

**Think of Elizabeth when:**

Your plans don't happen.

Someone's news overshadows you.

You are ignored.

Surprise guests visit for several months!

People say you are too old to......

*Herod the Great ruled over Judea, Samaria, Galilee, Perea, Idumea, Batanea (modern-day Syria), Gaza, Joppa, and parts of the coast. He was known for major construction projects, including the expanded Second Temple, desert fortresses, a major port city (Caesarea Maritima), and several palaces. He died when Jesus was about four years old and living in Egypt. The historian Josephus records Herod had at least nine wives, eunuch servants, and a reputation for a vicious temperament, paranoia, and violence.*

*Below is a map of Herod's territory divisions upon his death.*

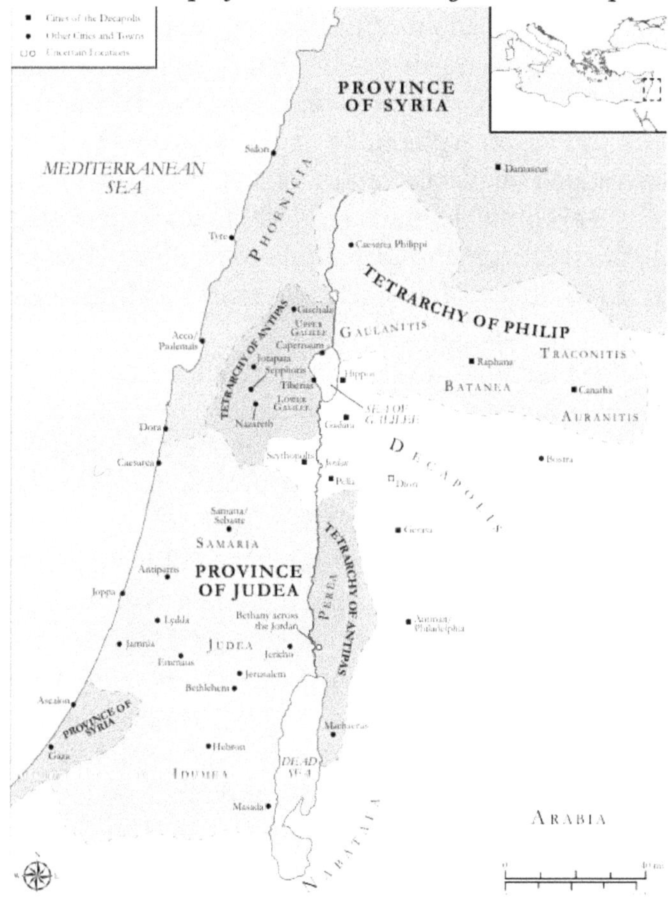


FreeBibleimages.org

# *Mary – The Early Years, Part 1*

Luke 1:26-56, 2:1-52

## Background:

Mary was a common name for women in the first century. The Hebrew form, Miriam, was the name of the prophetess and sister of Moses and Aaron. Scholars estimate that as many as 25% of Jewish women at the time were named Mary (Ilan, 1996, pp. 53–56).

The name may have meant "beloved" or "bitter." The interpretation of "bitter" could reflect the bitterness of slavery in Egypt during Miriam's time, or the burden of Roman occupation during Mary's life. It may also have expressed the difficult reality that daughters were more vulnerable and financially burdensome than sons, who added financial support to the family. Girls required protection and, eventually, marriage, often accompanied by a dowry to help provide for their future (Ilan, 1996, 88). In that sense, "bitter" may have reflected social hardship or cultural sorrow associated with raising daughters.

Over time, the meaning and emotional weight of the name Mary may have evolved, acquiring new associations and significance, especially through the life and legacy of the mother of Jesus.

Mary lived in Nazareth, a small agricultural village in Lower Galilee, likely home to no more than two to four hundred inhabitants in the first century. The Gospel of John suggests that Mary may have had a sister, noting that "standing near the cross of Jesus were his mother, and his mother's sister, Mary the wife of Clopas, and Mary Magdalene" (John 19:25). Some interpreters understand this verse to refer to two women named Mary, while others suggest that "his mother's sister" refers to Salome, who is named in Mark 15:40 and identified as the mother of James and John. If so, Mary and Salome may have been sisters, which would make James and John Jesus's cousins. Although certainty is impossible, such kinship connections were common in small Jewish communities.

Arranged marriages were typical in first-century culture, with girls commonly married between the ages of twelve and twenty-two

(Ilan, 1996, 59). Mary was betrothed (more binding than an engagement) to Joseph, and the length of the betrothal period often depended on the couple's ages, so we are not sure how long the arrangement was in place. While scripture does not specify Mary's age, most scholars believe she was likely in her teens, and based on her thoughtful responses and spiritual maturity, she may have been in her late teens or early twenties.

Mary appears to have been raised with a deep awareness of Jehovah and a strong grounding in Biblical history. Although women were not formally educated or included in Torah study, they could still receive instruction at home from their families (Ilan, 1996, 204). It is likely that Mary participated regularly in festivals and worship in Jerusalem. Her close relationship with her relative Elizabeth, who lived in the hill country of Judah, supports this assumption. In Luke 1:39, Mary is shown traveling there with confidence and purpose, suggesting that she had made the journey before and was well-acquainted with the route. Since women did not travel alone during this period. She likely went to Jerusalem with friends or relatives, then to Elizabeth's home.

Jephthah and his daughter

Among the customs Mary likely knew was the annual remembrance of Jephthah's daughter. For four days each year, Jewish women celebrated Jephthah's daughter, as mentioned in Judges 11:39–40. Jephthah had vowed to sacrifice whatever came out to greet him after his victory over the Ammonites. Tragically, his only child, his daughter, ran to meet him. When he explained his vow, her faithful response was:

*"My father, you have opened your mouth to the LORD;* ***do to me according to what has gone out of your mouth****, now*

*that the LORD has avenged you on your enemies, on the Ammonites." Judges 11:36.*

Jephthah's daughter willingly surrendered her life in obedience to the Lord, setting an example of devotion and sacrifice. Mary's own willingness to yield to God's will reflects this same spirit of faithfulness. (The full account of Jephthah's daughter is found in Judges 11.)

Matthew presents the birth narrative from Joseph's perspective and lineage, while Luke shares the story from Mary's point of view. Mary was a young woman, likely from the lineage of Nathan, a son of David and Bathsheba, assuming the genealogy in Luke 3 traces Mary's ancestry. She was betrothed to Joseph, who may have been originally from Bethlehem, as he identified with that town when traveling there to register for the Roman census.

## Mary: You will have a son: Luke 1:26-38

When Elizabeth was six months pregnant with John, the angel Gabriel appeared to Mary with a startling greeting: *"The Lord is with you; you are highly favored."* Mary was puzzled by this, but Gabriel reassured her that his message was one of good news.

She would conceive a son and name him Jesus, a name derived from Joshua, meaning *"Jehovah saves."* Though it was a common name at the time, Gabriel made it clear that this child would be unlike any other: He would be called the Son of the Most High, inheriting the throne of David, and His kingdom would never end.

Mary didn't question that the Messiah would be born or that she would be the mom, but responded with a practical question: *"How can this be, since I am a virgin?"* Gabriel explained that the Holy Spirit would come upon her, and the power of God would overshadow her. Because of this divine conception, the child would be called the Son of God.

When comparing Mary's acceptance of Gabriel's message to Zechariah's doubt, I think of how young people believe readily, while age can drag down our willingness to believe and change. Mary, the teen, accepted that she would be the mother of the Messiah, while Zechariah after years of waiting struggled to believe John would be born.

As a sign to confirm his message, Gabriel told Mary that her elder relative Elizabeth, long considered barren, was already six months pregnant, proof that *"nothing will be impossible with God."*

Mary's response to Gabriel's message, that she would miraculously conceive, reveals her deep humility and faith. She identifies herself as a servant of the Lord and submits to His will with words similar to another young girl response – Jephthah's daughter.

*... "May it be done to me according to your word." Luke 1:38*

Mary's words mirror the response of Jephthah's daughter, who accepted a future she did not choose, out of reverence and obedience to God. I suspect it was not a coincidence that Mary responded as Jephthah's daughter. It is encouraging to see the help we find from the examples provided in the Bible.

## *Reflection on Mary: You will have a son*

1. Mary asks how she will conceive since she is a virgin. What does that question tell you about Mary?

2. There is an old saying: Man plans, and God laughs. How do you feel when you have everything planned out and God changes it? How did Mary react?

3. From these few verses what are some of Mary's strengths?

# Mary visits Elizabeth: Luke 1:39-56

Mary hurried to visit Elizabeth, likely eager to confirm Gabriel's message and to support her older relative. While we know Mary believed the angel's words, unlike Zechariah who struggled to believe (Luke 1:45); she may have still longed to see the evidence of Elizabeth's miraculous pregnancy for herself. Imagine her excitement: Was Elizabeth truly expecting after all these years?

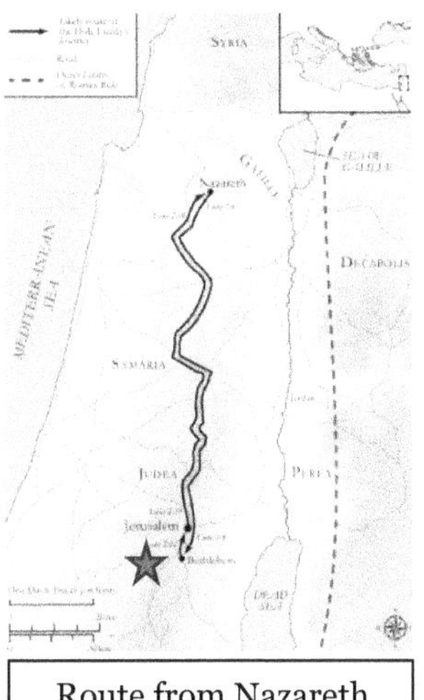

Route from Nazareth to Jerusalem.

This was a beautiful intergenerational friendship, the young Mary and the older Elizabeth, both experiencing unexpected pregnancies. From what we know of Elizabeth's warm and Spirit-filled greeting, Mary was welcomed with joy and affirmation. But how did Mary respond?

Her answer, recorded in Luke 1:46–55, reveals her heart and her faith. In what is often called the Magnificat, Mary breaks into a song of praise. Her words show a soaring spirit and a grateful soul, overwhelmed by what God has done. Echoing the poetic tradition of her ancestor David, Mary rejoices in God her Savior and acknowledges her humble position, marveling that generations will call her blessed.

She is both humbled and exultant, recognizing that the mighty God has done great things for her. Her praise celebrates God's holiness, His mercy to those who revere Him, and His power to overturn human pride and injustice. She declares God's frequent reversals where He:

- Scatters the proud,
- Brings down rulers and lifts up the lowly,
- Fills the hungry and sends the rich away empty.

Mary shares how God's ways are not ours. She concludes by affirming that God remembers His mercy, keeping His promises to Abraham and his descendants forever.

Mary's response reveals not only deep emotion but also a profound grasp of God's justice, power, and covenant faithfulness. Her words show notable faith and maturity for someone probably in their teens. Truly, Mary was a young woman of extraordinary understanding and devotion.

Mary stays with Elizabeth about three months before returning to Nazareth. Since Elizabeth was in her sixth month when Mary heard about her pregnancy, it's likely she stayed long enough to help with John's birth and perhaps even attend the circumcision eight days later. What a great opportunity to learn for someone who will not have a midwife or the help from other women when she later gives birth in a stable.

If Mary did attend the circumcision, she would have heard Zechariah speak for the first time since losing his voice, likely sharing his powerful encounter with Gabriel. These months must have been deeply encouraging for Mary, especially during her first trimester. Both Elizabeth and Zechariah, a priestly household, recognized her child as the Lord, and their own son as His forerunner.

Though Scripture doesn't tell us what Elizabeth and Mary discussed, we can imagine their conversations were rich with awe, faith, and shared wonder. Before Mary left Nazareth, she may have shared Gabriel's words with her family. Did others believe she was pregnant with the Messiah? Would you believe a teen girl who told you she was pregnant with the Messiah? But with Elizabeth and Zechariah, Mary lived for a short time with a righteous, priestly family who knew the truth and supported her.

Mary probably learned more about Zechariah's encounter with Gabriel and Elizabeth validated Gabriel's message about her pregnancy. She would share Elizabeth's joy and help with the house while Elizabeth dealt with the last trimester and birth. Mary might have had doubts about the future, but Zechariah and Elizabeth's life and blessings would have been very encouraging to a young woman on an unknown path! They would provide reassurance in their recognition of her child's divine birth. It helps when someone believes you, and Mary would have found that support with Elizabeth and Zechariah.

Elizabeth would probably appreciate Mary's calm and practical approach. Mary may have helped quelch any doubts or fears of Elizabeth. Sometimes older parents worry they will not be there to raise their children to adulthood. With shorter lifespans in New Testament times, it could have been a concern for Elizabeth. Seeing how God has planned John and Jesus's births may have encouraged Elizabeth to trust more and worry less.

In Elizabeth, Mary found support and belief that her pregnancy was from God. Mary likely cherished her time in their home, a unique season of mutual support between a young expectant mother and an older, faithful couple.

After all, even Benjamin Franklin reminded us in 1736: *"Fish and visitors stink after three days."* Mary stayed for three months, a testament to the welcome and warmth she must have received.

## *Reflections on Mary visits Elizabeth*

1. Why did Mary hurry to visit Elizabeth after Gabriel's message?

2. Visiting someone uninvited for 3 months: What kind of friendship did Mary and Elizabeth share?

3. What insight does Mary's response (Magnificat) to Elizabeth give us about her heart and faith?

4. What are some strengths Mary exhibited in these passages? Did you see any weaknesses?

## Mary back to Nazareth: Matthew 1:18-25

Once Mary is back in Nazareth, Joseph discovers that Mary is pregnant, and he knows the child is not his. If Mary had already shared with him what the angel Gabriel had told her, Joseph clearly didn't believe. He planned to end the engagement quietly to spare her public disgrace (Matthew 1:18–19).

Under the Law (Deuteronomy 22:23–24), Mary could have faced severe consequences, even stoning, since her condition would suggest unfaithfulness during betrothal. But God intervened. A messenger of the Lord appeared to Joseph in a dream, confirming that Mary's story was true, that her child was conceived by the Holy Spirit. Joseph responded in obedience and took Mary as his wife, but they remained sexually abstinent until after Jesus's birth, as recorded in Matthew 1:20–25.

For about six months, Mary and Joseph shared a very unusual relationship. As Mary's pregnancy became more visible, it would have been obvious to others that the pregnancy timeline didn't align with their marriage. Joseph likely endured whispers and judgment, accused of either impropriety before marriage or foolishness for marrying a woman carrying another man's child. For a man known for his righteousness, being misjudged as unrighteous must have been deeply frustrating. (And human nature being what it is, it's fair to assume that gossip circulated then as it would now.)

Meanwhile, Mary was navigating the emotional and physical toll of pregnancy—hormonal changes, social pressure, and the responsibility of carrying the Son of God. And Joseph, with faith and quiet strength, accepted his role as her protector, companion, and guardian.

### *Reflections on Mary back to Nazareth*

1. How would you feel if the girl you were to marry tells you she is pregnant miraculously?

2. What did Mary face as a single pregnant girl?

3. Describe what Joseph and Mary's relationship would have been for the six months before going to Bethlehem?

## Mary to Bethlehem: Luke 2:1-21

Because of a Roman decree for a census, Joseph was required to travel to Bethlehem, his ancestral town. Mary, ever practical, likely anticipated the possibility of giving birth along the way. She had probably witnessed or even assisted with other births before, possibly helping Elizabeth. When the time came, she and Joseph welcomed their son in the humblest of settings, a barn or cave used to shelter animals and laid Him in a manger as His first cradle. It is an unexpected way for the Son of God to come, but they are isolated and safe. Despite stories of talking animals and helpful drummers at a friendly barn, the reality was likely far more uncomfortable. Luke 2:1-7.

After the exhaustion of travel, the disappointment of having no room at the inn, and the difficulty of giving birth in a stable, Mary is soon joined by visitors. Out in the fields, shepherds had received a stunning message from an angel: the Messiah had been born and could be found lying in a manger. A multitude of heavenly hosts had praised God, declaring:

> *"Glory to God in the highest, and on earth peace among people with whom He is pleased." Luke 2:14*

The shepherds came and found Mary, Joseph, and the baby, just as the angel had said. They shared all that had been revealed to them, affirming the divine nature of the child.

Mary treasured these words, holding them deeply in her heart (Luke 2:8–21). This quiet reflection will become a pattern in her life.

### *Reflections on Mary to Bethlehem*

1. Luke 2:1-5 explains Joseph went to Bethlehem to register for the census, but why did a very pregnant Mary go with him?

2. Mary treasured what the shepherds shared in her heart (Luke 2:19). What were the points from the shepherd's story you would put in your child's scrapbook?

## Mary at the Temple: Luke 2:22-38

Eight days after His birth, the baby is circumcised and officially named Jesus, in obedience to the angel's instructions. Later, Mary and Joseph bring Him to the temple in Jerusalem to present Him as their firstborn son and to offer the required sacrifice. According to Leviticus 12:6–8, the ideal offering was a lamb, but a pair of doves or pigeons was permitted for those who couldn't afford one. Their offering of two birds suggests that Joseph and Mary were of modest means, introducing the reality that Jesus would be raised in a humble, frugal home (Luke 2:22–24).

At the temple, they encounter a righteous and devout man named Simeon, who takes the child in his arms and declares that he can now die in peace, for he has seen the Messiah with his own eyes. Simeon blesses them and proclaims that Jesus is the salvation of God, a light of revelation for the Gentiles and the glory of Israel. While Elizabeth had been the first to privately recognize Jesus as Lord, Simeon publicly announces His identity in the temple (Luke 2:25–35).

But Simeon also turns to Mary with a sobering prophecy. He tells her that many in Israel will fall and rise because of her son. Jesus will bring transformation, but not without conflict. Though Mary may have already sensed how difficult belief in miracles could be, Simeon confirms it: signs alone will not convince everyone. Her son will be opposed, and a sword will pierce her own soul. What's more, the true condition of people's hearts will be revealed in how they respond to Him.

At this moment, Mary is likely filled with awe and joy, hearing others proclaim her son as the Messiah. She and Joseph are amazed by what is spoken over Jesus. But Simeon gives her reason to pause. The path ahead will not be easy. Jesus is indeed salvation, but He will also expose sin, endure rejection, and ultimately cause deep sorrow for Mary herself.

There was more joy at the temple when Anna, a prophetess from the tribe of Asher, approached Mary, Joseph, and the child. She gave thanks to God and began to proclaim the good news to everyone who was waiting for the redemption of Jerusalem, the

Redeemer had come (Luke 2:36–38). Anna's focus was clear: Jerusalem now had a Redeemer, and the long-awaited hope of salvation had arrived.

Simeon and Anna both responded to God first before sharing their message with others. Simeon reveals Jesus as the Messiah and the cost of His ministry, while Anna announces the fulfillment of hope, the Redeemer has come. Two witnesses, two prophets, one male, one female, both old- declaring Jesus's role in our future. (Jewish laws required two witnesses, Deuteronomy 19:15, 17:6.)

## *Reflections on Mary at the Temple*

1. Mary and Joseph follow Moses' law and offer doves as a sacrifice for their firstborn. Most assume it indicates a family that is not wealthy enough to have a lamb to offer. What would be the pros and cons for Jesus to be raised in a wealthy or frugal home?

2. How would you expect Mary to react after her day at the Temple with Jesus?

## Mary lives in Bethlehem: Matthew 2:1-12

Matthew includes the time after Jesus's birth when Joseph, Mary, and Jesus remained in Bethlehem. Maybe Joseph and Mary were seeking a 'fresh start' in his hometown. They had experienced a lot of changes since Gabriel first appeared to Mary. She had become miraculously pregnant, traveled to the hill country of Judah, heard Elizabeth proclaim her unborn child as the Lord, formed a companionship with Joseph, made the long journey to Bethlehem, given birth, received a visit from shepherds (with no mention of drummers), heard Simeon and Anna publicly declare her son as the Savior and Redeemer and settled in a house in Bethlehem.

Then after recognizing an astonishing sign: a star marking the arrival of the Messiah. Wise men from the East, set out to find the newborn King. While the Old Testament does not clearly reference a star linked directly to the Messiah, Numbers 24:17, spoken by Balaam, has often been interpreted as a Messianic prophecy:

> *"A star shall come out of Jacob, and a scepter shall rise out of Israel..."*

Although Old Testament prophecy primarily centers on God's communication with Israel, Scripture reveals that God's heart has also extended beyond the descendants of Abraham. The story of Jonah, for example, shows how God sent a prophet to Assyria, where the people and even the king repented, fasted, and turned to God (Jonah 3:6–10).

As David writes in Psalm 145:18:

> *"The LORD is near to all who call on Him, to all who call on Him in truth."*

The visit of the Magi is a powerful reminder that God's salvation was never meant for Israel alone, but for all who seek Him in truth. God is not exclusive to the children of Abraham, though Scripture primarily records His interactions with Israel. We are simply not told His communication with others. Yet the wise men from the East clearly had some knowledge of the Messiah, and they set out with a desire to worship Him. They followed the signs and eventually sought further guidance from Herod the Great. After learning from the religious leaders that the Messiah was to be born in Bethlehem, the star guided them to the place where Mary and Jesus were staying. (Note that the religious leaders were not interested in a potential Messiah in Bethlehem.)

This was no brief journey. The Magi expended time, preparation, and significant cost. But God led them to Jesus. They bowed in worship and presented their gifts of gold (royalty), frankincense (divinity), and myrrh (suffering and burial). These offerings reflected their understanding of Jesus's mission. The wise men were warned in a dream not to return to Herod, and they obeyed, returning home by another route (Matthew 2:1–12).

While we talk about the wise men at Jesus's birth, they visit Mary at the house they were staying, not at a stable or manger. Jesus is not referred to as a baby by Matthew, but child. Herod when he realizes the magi had tricked him, boys two years old and under are killed in Bethlehem indicating a span of time from the birth and the visit of the Magi that Jesus has spent in Bethlehem. The wise men were the first Gentiles to worship Jesus, representing the nations beyond Israel. They bowed to a child with no throne, no army and no crown. As a Gentile, I'm moved by their devotion and their connection with God. Mary has Gentiles in her home and again sees others worship and praise her son. She must have felt so blessed! A righteous husband and a son that people come from different countries to worship and bring gifts! But while it was a season of blessing and wonder, trouble was drawing near, and life was about to take a difficult turn.

Jesus is announced across every realm and every boundary—by the heavens, by a star, by angels, by male and female prophets, by the rich and the poor, by Jews and by Gentiles. Gabriel speaks to Mary before conception. Elizabeth recognizes the Messiah in the womb. Angels proclaim His birth and shepherds worship a newborn in the stable. Simeon and Anna testify over Him at His dedication in the Temple. The Magi journey from distant lands to worship the child in His home.

Before Jesus ever preaches a word, heaven has testified. The Spirit has testified. The righteous remnant of Israel has testified. The nations have testified and Mary is a witness to them all.

## *Reflections on Mary lives in Bethlehem*

1. What do the actions of the wise men suggest about their relationship with God?

2. In Acts 10:28 Peter expresses his concern about associating or visiting a Gentile with Cornelius. This suggest that first century devout Jews would be resistant to share a meal or entertain Gentiles in their homes. In Galatians 2:11-14 Paul addresses Peter's continued resistance, although he finally overcame his bias. How did Mary react to Gentiles (the wise men) coming into her home?

## Mary lives in Egypt: Matthew 2: 13-18

After the wise men departed, a messenger of the Lord appeared to Joseph in a dream, warning him to leave Bethlehem immediately. The message was urgent; Jesus's life was in danger. Joseph didn't hesitate. He rose that very night, gathered Mary and the child, and they fled to Egypt. There is no mention of how the gifts Jesus received were used, but if they needed funds to hide from Herod, they received them just in time.

Meanwhile, Herod, realizing the wise men had outwitted him, became enraged. To eliminate any threat to his rule from a king, he ordered the massacre of all boys two years old and under in Bethlehem and its surrounding areas (Matthew 2:16–18). With no rapid communication systems in place, Joseph and Mary may not have known what had happened. Likely disconnected from their families, they relied entirely on God's guidance for when it was safe to return.

After Herod the Great's death, Joseph received another dream—it was time to return to Israel. As they journey back, they hear that Herod's son Archelaus has control of Judea. Joseph may have been planning to return to Bethlehem. Once again, Joseph is warned in a dream, and they chose to settle in Mary's hometown of Nazareth in Galilee (Matthew 2:19-23).

## *Reflections on Mary lives in Egypt*

1. How might Egypt have influenced Mary's understanding of Simeon's warning?

## Mary settles back in Nazareth

Matthew 13:55-56; Luke 2:41–52

The exact length of the family's stay in Egypt is unknown, but it was likely no more than a couple of years. By the time they returned to Galilee, Mary may have had a deeper understanding of Simeon's warning that her son would be a source of division and fear for some. Given the threats, the family likely kept quiet about Jesus's true identity. In many ways, they were hiding, quietly building a life in the rural town of Nazareth.

Life probably settled into a rhythm of normalcy. Mary and Joseph went on to have other children. Matthew 13:55–56 names James, Joseph, Simon, Judas, and mentions sisters as part of Jesus's physical family. Since James is listed first, he may have been the eldest after Jesus, Joseph's first biological son.

While we imagine they were good children, it wouldn't have been easy growing up with an older brother who was kind, wise, and without fault. Sibling rivalry is a common part of family life, and Jesus's perfection may have created tension among the others. One can imagine Mary wrestling with the challenges of parenting, knowing that her firstborn was the Son of God, while trying not to show favoritism toward Him among a household of very human children who bickered, argued, and tested her limits.

Mary lived in Nazareth, Judah, Bethlehem, Egypt, and again in Nazareth over the course of three to four years. Eventually, she and Joseph established their home in the quiet village of Nazareth, among her people. There, they worked, played, attended synagogue, and traveled each year to Jerusalem for the Feast of the Passover.

When Jesus was twelve, the family made their usual pilgrimage to Jerusalem. On the return journey, they assumed Jesus was traveling with the group. Mary may have had six or more children to wrangle on the trip. After a day's travel, they realized He was missing and anxiously retraced their steps. For three days, they searched Jerusalem, asking relatives and friends if they had seen Him.

Finally, they found Him in the temple, sitting among the teachers, listening and asking questions. The teachers were amazed at His understanding. Mary, filled with anxiety and relief, scolded Jesus for causing them such worry. But His reply revealed something deeper; He expected them to know where He would be. Even at twelve, Jesus was aware of His identity and mission. Mary, however, did not yet grasp the full meaning of His calling or how it would unfold.

Still, Jesus returned with them to Nazareth and was obedient. Luke tells us again that Mary treasured all these things in her heart (Luke 2:41–52).

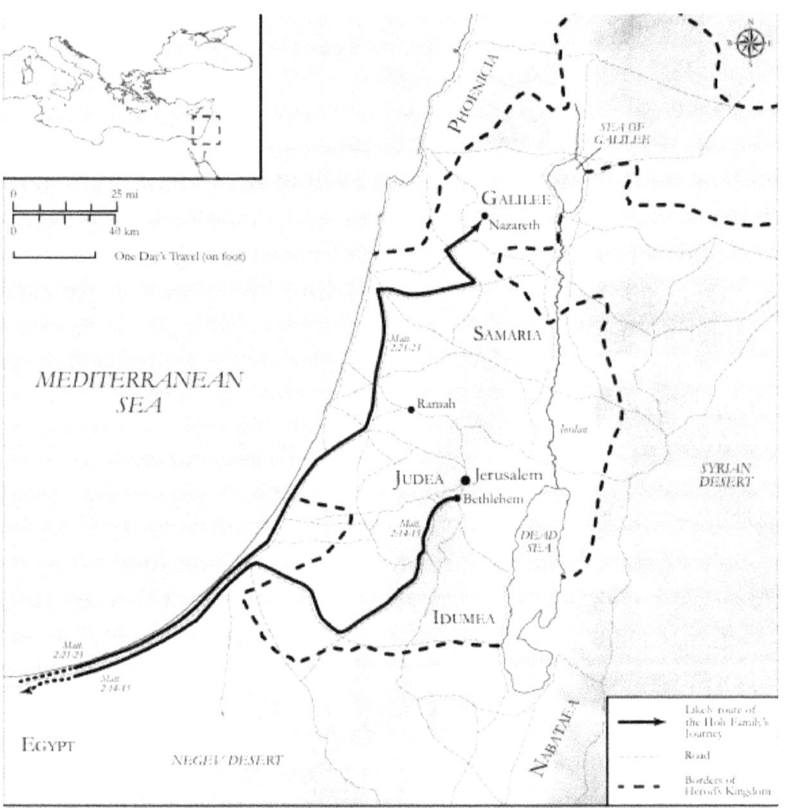

From Bethlehem to Egypt then to Nazareth

## *Reflections on Mary settles back in Nazareth*

1. What was life in Nazareth like for Mary and Joseph?

2. What do you think were the challenges and benefits of having Jesus and several siblings?

3. How has Mary learned to depend to God?

4. What are some of Mary's strengths that we can emulate?

5. What weaknesses did Mary show that we should be aware of in ourselves?

**Think of Mary the Early Years when:**

You struggle to be obedient to the Lord.

You want to hear a song of praise.

You hate to relocate.

What else would you add?

# *Anna*

Luke 2:36-38

There was a prophet, Anna, of the tribe of Asher at the temple in Jerusalem when Mary, Joseph and Jesus come to the temple.

While Elizabeth was the first to prophecy about the arrival of the Messiah, Anna praises God for the Redeemer. She is honored as one of the last prophets from the Old Covenant, in the line of Miriam, Deborah and Huldah. A member of the tribe of Asher her ancestors probably migrated to Judah before the Assyrians took the Northern Kingdom away. We do not know if she prophesied prior to Jesus's appearance or if this is her only message.

We know she was about 84 years old, which in the first century would be ancient. Luke tells us she remained single after her husband died. If she was 20 at marriage and her husband died at 27, Anna would have focused her time and energy on seeking the Redeemer of Isreal by prayer and fasting for 57 years. This is a guess, it could have been longer or less, but it was a significant portion of her life.

Some suggest Anna could have taken a vow of the Nazarene. Luke doesn't mention Anna as a Nazarene but shares her actions. A Nazarene was a man or woman who vow to separate themselves unto Jehovah (Numbers 6:2). They had diet and grooming restrictions and could not do anything that would make them unclean. When the time of the vow is completed the actions to end the vow is explained in Numbers 6:13-21. It was not a lifelong restriction, but one for a period of time. Whether Anna took a vow or not, she spent most of her life at the temple praying, fasting and seeking the promised Redeemer.

Widows were often seen as vulnerable and in need of care with several passages mentioning their needs: James 1:27, 1 Timothy 5:3-16, Acts 6:1-6, Luke 20:47, and Mark 12:40. While remarriage was encouraged, widows who chose singleness for spiritual dedication could be honored. Anna exemplifies a 'solitary servant,' using her widowhood to seek God with purpose.[1] Her passion was the coming of the Redeemer:

> *"A Redeemer will come to Zion, And to those in Jacob who turn from wrongdoing," declares the LORD (Isaiah 59:20).*

When Jesus is brought to the temple as a baby, Anna's first response is to give thanks to God! The Redeemer had arrived! Then she told everyone who were looking for the redemption of Jerusalem about Jesus. Anna announced at the temple that the Redeemer had appeared! Simeon, from Jerusalem, witnessed to those at the temple that Jesus was the Messiah. Anna from the northern tribe of Israel provided the second witness of Jesus's mission. While Simeon focused on Jesus's mission and suffering, Anna's message is hope-filled redemption.

Anna's passion was seeking the Redeemer. As a young woman, she wanted to see the Messiah that would redeem Isreal. She spent most of her life fasting as part of her service. It's not likely that she didn't eat at all but fasted during select hours or did partial fasts such as Daniel and limited her food choices (Daniel 10:3). Secondly, she prayed. This wasn't a prayer on the way to work or before bed. These were hours spent praying every day. Finally, she chose to share her passion publicly, at the temple. She didn't sit in her recliner and pray. She went out among people and prayed. If you went to the temple, would you see Anna? You probably would. You knew she would be there praying and fasting. She never gave up. Sometimes it is easier, as you age to sit and expect others to come to you, but Anna went out every day and her actions showed her passion. After decades, God answered her prayers - she saw the Redeemer!

---

[1] Jesus mentions those who made themselves eunuchs (single servants) for the sake of the kingdom of heaven in Matthew 19:12. Anna seems to be someone who fit this description.

## *Reflection on Anna*

1. If you went to the temple and saw Anna, what would you think?

2. What did Anna not do?

3. Describe what you feel are Anna's strengths?

4. What were some possible limitations for Anna?

**Think of Anna when:**

You don't think prayer is powerful.

Prayer and fasting are the only actions you can do to help.

After a time with no answer, you get discouraged.

God answers your prayer.

# *Jesus – The Early Years*

*While this study focuses on women of the New Testament, it is impossible to not discuss Jesus. Gabriel tells Mary He will be called the Son of the Most High (Luke 1:32). While pregnant, Elizabeth and John recognize Him as my Lord (Luke 1:43). After His birth, the Heavenly Host call Him a Savior, who is Christ the Lord (Luke 2:11), the shepherds worship Him as the promised Messiah. Simeon calls Him a light for revelation to the Gentiles and the glory of Israel (Luke 2:32), while Anna announces the Redeemer has arrived. Gentiles came a long distance to worship and bring gifts for a divine king who will suffer.*

*It's striking to observe who recognize Jesus: a priestly family (Elizabeth and Zechariah), heavenly beings, humble shepherds, a devout Jerusalemite (Simeon), a faithful northern exile (Anna), and foreign Gentiles from the East. Each group represents a different class, region, or nation, united by their recognition of the Messiah.*

*Just as conspicuous is the absence of others: Herod the Great, the Pharisees, Sadducees, and scribes, are nowhere among those who worshipped Him. Even when prophets like Simeon and Anna announce Him at the temple, the leaders didn't acknowledge Him.*

*Jesus spent His early years in Bethlehem, fled with His family to Egypt, and was raised in Nazareth. Herod was the first to seek His life, a threat that foreshadowed the opposition He would face throughout His ministry.*

If you are curious about the government at this time, the appendix has some background information about the Herodians and Roman rulers.

# *Mary at the wedding Part 2*

John 2:1-12

Jesus had begun to teach and gather disciples—John, Andrew, Peter, Philip, and Nathanael (John 1:29–51). Word was already spreading about Him. Not far from Nazareth, a wedding was being celebrated in Cana of Galilee, a village about a two-hour walk away (5-6 miles). Jesus was there with His new followers, and Mary, His mother.

In the middle of the celebration, Mary noticed that the wine had run out, an embarrassment for the hosts. She quietly approached Jesus and informed Him, "They have no wine." It was a simple statement. She didn't ask for anything directly, but Jesus understood what she was implying.

His response sounds almost abrupt: "Woman, what does this have to do with Me? My hour has not yet come." There is no disrespect, only clarity that His timing was not now. However, Mary seemed to know her son, she had spent over 30 years with Him. Mary must have had some understanding that Jesus would be able to help with the lack of wine. She didn't argue or press. Instead, she turned to the servants and simply said, "Do whatever He tells you." That trust, Mary's quiet confidence in Jesus's compassion and power is striking. No drama, no persuasion. Just faith that He would help.

Jesus then instructed the servants to fill six large stone jars used for ceremonial washing, each holding about thirty gallons, with water. Once filled, He told them to draw some drink and take it to the master of the feast. The water had become wine - good wine. So good that the host remarked that it was unusual to serve the best last.

This quiet miracle, performed without spectacle, stands as the first recorded sign of Jesus. Yet it may not have been the first time He quietly stepped in to help when needed. Mary seemed to know her Son well, trusting both His compassion and His ability to act at the right moment.

After the wedding, Jesus left with His mother, His brothers, James, Joseph, Simon, and Judas, and His disciples. They traveled together to Capernaum, a town near the Sea of Galilee, and stayed there for a few days. It was a small pause before the public ministry began.

## *Reflections on Mary at the wedding*

1. What does Mary's response to the servants, "Do whatever He tells you", tell us about her understanding of Jesus?

2. What are some possible reasons Mary knew Jesus would help?

3. What lessons can we learn from Mary's example when we encounter a need or a problem? How can we imitate her posture of faith and her simple direction: "Do whatever He tells you"?

4. How did Jesus honor his mother (Exodus 20:12, Deuteronomy 5:16, Matthew 15:3-6, Mark 7:9-13, Matthew 19:17-19, Mark 10:19: Luke 18:20).

**Think of Mary when:**

You need to trust God.

*From Capernaum, Jesus traveled to Jerusalem to observe the Passover, as was the custom. He removes the merchants from the temple, meets with Nicodemus and teaches. Jesus remained in the region of Judea for a time, teaching and spending time with His disciples.*

*John the Baptist was still active nearby, calling people to repentance and baptizing those who responded. Initially, the focus remained on John, but as Jesus taught, He drew more followers. Eventually, the attention of the Pharisees began to shift toward Him.*

*Sensing the growing scrutiny, Jesus chose to return north to Galilee. Rather than taking the long route around, He traveled directly through Samaria, a region most Jews avoided.*

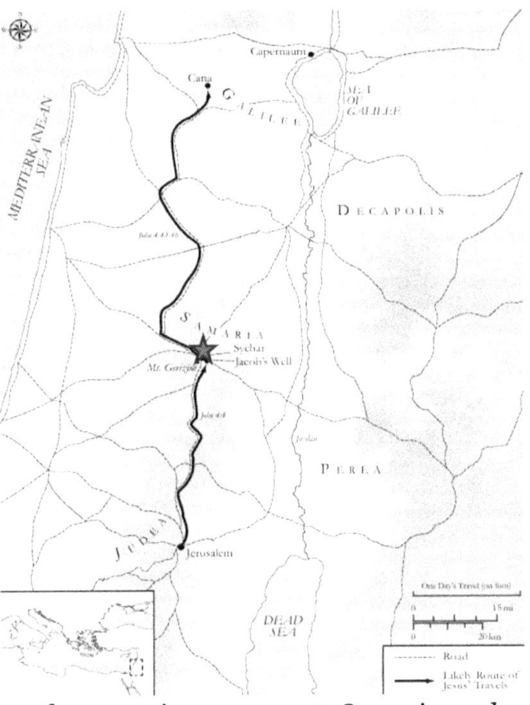


*Tension existed between the Jews and the Samaritans. The Samaritan people were believed to be descendants of the northern tribes of Israel who had remained in the land after the Assyrian conquest. Over time, they had intermarried with foreigners and developed distinct religious practices. Though they worshiped the same God, Jehovah, they considered Mount Gerizim, not Jerusalem, to be an acceptable place of worship (John 4:20).*

*Weary from travel, Jesus stopped to rest at a well near the Samaritan village of Sychar. While He sat alone, His disciples went into the town to buy food.*

# *Samaritan woman*

John 4:1-42

Jesus traveling from Judea to Galilee stops at Jacob's well, a link to ancestral covenants. Around midday, as Jesus rested by the well, a Samaritan woman came to draw water. Jesus begins a conversation by asking her for a drink. Her response:

> *"How is it that You, though You are a Jew, are asking me for a drink, though I am a Samaritan woman?" John 4:9.*

Her response could be interpreted as skeptical, surprised, or even defensive. Jews typically avoided contact with Samaritans, especially women, and she likely expected Him to do the same. (A Samaritan woman would be treated as unclean by some and taking water from her would also make the recipient unclean (Ilan, 1996, 103,105)). Jesus, ignoring gender and ethnic boundaries, seems to ignore her response and tells her that He is not ordinary. He appeals to her curiosity with three statements:

- if you knew the gift of God,
- if you knew who is speaking to you
- if you had asked then you could have received living water.

The woman responds with both respect and practicality. She addresses Him as "Sir" and points out the obvious: He has no bucket, and the well is deep. Where, then, would this "living water" come from? She follows her question with another, does He think He's greater than their ancestor Jacob, who gave them the well?

Rather than getting sidetracked into a debate about Jacob and ancestry, Jesus keeps the focus on the water. He agrees with the woman that the well provides temporary relief, but what He offers is far greater, a spring of water welling up to eternal life. Jesus evokes Isaiah 12:3, "with joy shall you draw water out of the wells of salvation". Intrigued, the woman asks for this water, probably hoping to avoid daily trips to the well.

Again, Jesus changes the direction of the conversation. He tells her to call her husband. This pivot seems abrupt, but it leads her to a personal moment of confession. She replies, "I have no husband," to which Jesus encourages her honesty, revealing that He knows her full history: five previous husbands, and the man she's now with is not her husband. This is someone who had apparently been divorced five times, and the man she was living with was not willing to marry her. She had endured broken covenant relationships. She didn't come to the well with other women, but alone at mid-day, indicating her isolation. With five marriages, no children mentioned, she appears to have had a difficult life. And Jesus understood her past and her struggles. He knew her sins and invited her to drink living water.

Whether this is the full exchange or only the essential parts, we don't know, but her next statement shows growing realization: "Sir, I perceive that You are a prophet." Again, she tries to discuss their different understanding of worship. And again, Jesus deflects her question. Instead, He explains that God is Spirit, and true worshippers must revere the Father in spirit and in truth.

Her response at this point is that the Messiah will come and tell us all things. Jesus then makes a rare declaration: "I am." He identifies Himself clearly as the Messiah. This lowly Samaritan woman was the first person recorded that Jesus plainly tells he is the Messiah.

And like any great story, at that moment, the disciples return, interrupting the discussion. They were surprised to find Him speaking with a woman, let alone a Samaritan. John contrasts his and the disciple's prejudice to Jesus's inclusion of the struggling and ignored.

The woman, overcome with excitement, leaves her waterpot behind and hurries into the city. She begins to tell the men in the village about Jesus. Her testimony is compelling enough that many come out to see Jesus for themselves. Her joy at finding Jesus is contagious. If people shunned her before, her testimony brought others to Him.

As a result of her witness, many in Sychar believed in Him. They invited Jesus to stay, and He remained with them two days. During that time, even more people came to believe; not just because of the woman's words, but because they heard Jesus themselves and were convinced, He was the Messiah.

## *Reflections on the Samaritan Woman*

1. When others believed because of her testimony about Jesus, what does that imply about the Samaritan woman?

2. If we assume it was not a coincidence that Jesus was alone by the well when the woman came (or Jesus knew she would be there and sent his followers away). Why would Jesus seek her out?

3. What are some strengths from this woman we should emulate?

4. Are there weaknesses we should recognize to avoid?

**Think of the Samaritan woman when:**

You have an opportunity to tell others about Jesus

You think your life is too messy for Jesus to care.

# *Peter's mother-in-law*

*Matthew 8:14–17; Mark 1:29–34; Luke 4:38–41*

Jesus returns to Galilee teaching and performing miracles in Cana, but when He visits Nazareth, He refuses to perform signs and wonders simply to satisfy their demands. Meanwhile, John the Baptist was imprisoned by Herod Antipas while Jesus settles in Capernaum.

On one Sabbath, Jesus and His disciples went to the synagogue, where He taught and healed a man possessed by an unclean spirit. Afterward, they went to the home of Peter and Andrew. Peter's mother-in-law lay sick with a fever. The disciples were concerned enough to tell Jesus about her condition. He went to her, took her by the hand, helped her up, and the fever left her. A second healing on the Sabbath, one public, one private. In response, she got up and began to serve them.

Peter's mother-in-law is mentioned in all three Synoptic Gospels. She lived with her daughter and Peter, and the disciples were clearly concerned about her well-being. When Jesus healed her, her immediate response was one of gratitude expressed through service, a reflection of a servant's heart.

## *Reflections on Peter's mother-in-law*

1. What are we to learn from this story about Peter's mother-in-law?

**Think of Peter's mother-in-law when:**

Someone helps you and you want to return their kindness.

*Jesus performed many works throughout Galilee: casting out demons, healing Peter's mother-in-law of a fever, cleansing a leper, enabling a paralytic to walk, and restoring both the lame and a man with a withered hand. In Capernaum a Roman centurion, recognizing Jesus' power, asked Jewish elders to request healing for his servant. As Jesus approached, the centurion sent word that He need not come in person, only speak the word, and the servant would be healed since he was not worthy to have Jesus in his home. Jesus's power went beyond physical presence.*

*In addition to these miracles, Jesus taught constantly revealing His insights in the law and practical matters. Luke records His awareness of a widow's grief at the loss of her only son.*

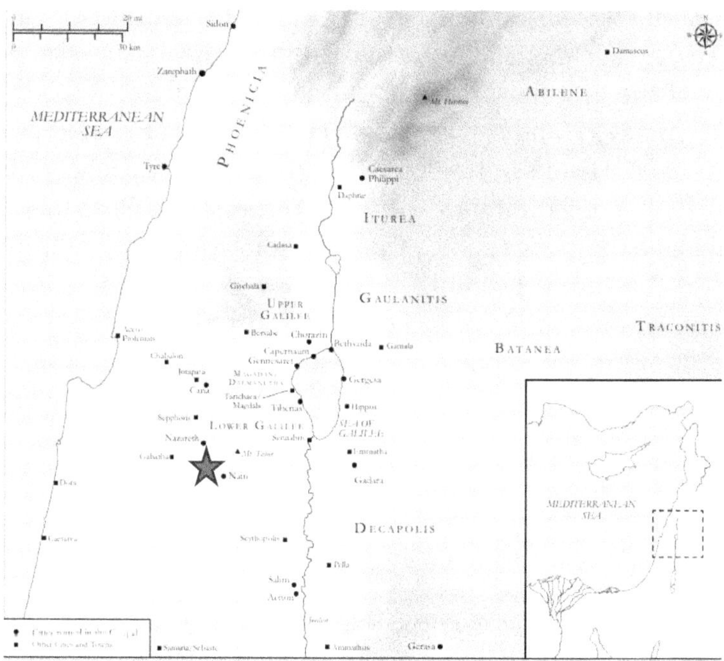


*The map shows the town of Nain, where Jesus helps another widow.*

# *Widow of Nain*

Luke 7:11-17

The town of Nain lies about 25 miles southwest of Capernaum, an uphill journey that would have taken Jesus and His followers 8 to 10 hours on foot. Situated near a major trade route through the Jezreel Valley, Nain was strategically located.

The burial of a young man probably followed Jewish customs. According to Mosaic Law, anyone who touched a dead body would be ceremonially unclean for seven days. This would entail isolation, washing clothes, bathing and sprinkling with water purified by the priests on certain days (Numbers 19). Only immediate family members were permitted to handle the dead (Leviticus 21:1–3). Therefore, it would be unexpected for outsiders to approach a dead body. Burial was also quick. No embalming or waiting for traveling relatives. As such, burial was often on the same day, as seen in the stories of the prophet in 1 Kings 13:29–30, Saul and his sons in 1 Samuel 31:11–13, and even Ananias and Sapphira in Acts 5:6, 10.

As Jesus, His disciples, and a large crowd approached the gate of Nain, they encountered a funeral procession. Probably not a coincidence that Jesus comes from a 9 hour walk just as the body is going to the burial grounds. A widow was mourning the recent death of her only child, and a large crowd from Nain were with her. He felt her grief and approached her with compassion saying, "Do not continue to weep." Then, He touched the bier carrying the young man—an act that halted the procession. Jesus spoke to the dead man, "Young man, I say to you, arise." Immediately, the young man sat up and began to speak. Jesus then gave him to his mother.

Those who witnessed the miracle, both the crowd traveling with Jesus and the mourners accompanying the widow, were overwhelmed with awe and glorified God. They might have recalled another miraculous moment hundreds of years earlier that had taken place about a mile away in Shunem, where the prophet Elisha raised the Shunammite woman's son from the dead (2 Kings 4). By raising the widow's son, Jesus would have echoed the prophets in action and location. The people recognizing Jesus's power, proclaim

Him a great prophet and news of this astounding resurrection spread rapidly throughout the surrounding region.

## *Reflections on the Widow of Nain*

1. It seems that Jesus made this trek to help this widow. While Luke does not provide any specific reason, Why would this widow be the one Jesus helped?

2. We don't have the widow's reaction or much about her. We only have how the people supported her and Jesus's actions. Do you see any strength to remember?

**Think of the Widow of Nain when:**

You are overwhelmed with grief, and not sure if God cares.

# *Weeping Sinner*

Luke 7:36-50

Jesus was gaining a reputation as both a teacher and a prophet. One of the Pharisees, named Simon, invited Him to his home for a meal and conversation. In New Testament culture, prominent homes often featured open courtyards where members of the community could gather and listen in. Jesus's visit must have been well publicized, as a woman from the city, known for her sinful life, came intentionally, bringing a jar of perfume to anoint Him. As Jesus reclined at the table, the woman approached His feet. Overwhelmed, she began to weep so profusely that her tears washed the dirt from His feet. Without a towel, she used her hair to dry them. Kissing His feet, she did what she came for, anointing him with the perfume. She didn't come to be healed from a physical issue or to tell him about her need for money or justice. She came for forgiveness. This sinner recognized Jesus was more than a prophet healing the physically sick. While others came to Jesus for free food or to heal their servants or loved ones, she was the first mentioned who comes to Jesus in humble repentance.

Jesus understood the Pharisee's heart as he watched the woman and talks about a topic that Simon would appreciate – money. He described two debtors, one who owed a small amount, the other a large sum, neither of whom could repay their debt. The lender forgave both, giving each a new start.

Then Jesus posed a behavioral question: Would the debtors' reaction differ? In other words: Who would appreciate the cancellation of the debt the most? Would the amount forgiven change a person's reaction? The woman knows she is a large debtor, Simon does not believe he is. Jesus answers with a truism: The greater the debt forgiven the greater the appreciation.

Jesus contrasts the woman's acts of washing, drying, kissing and anointing Him with Simon's neglect of hospitality. Simon and this sinner showed how they valued Jesus with their actions. Simon felt he had few debts and therefore showed little love. The woman realized she was a sinner. Her actions show her love and hope that Jesus would be gracious. Her tears revealed an outpouring of repentance. Jesus sees her faith and responds with forgiveness and mercy. She finally has peace.

Simon doesn't know he is a sinner and acts accordingly: no water for feet, no kiss, no oil. The weeping woman realized her debt and comes to Jesus with perfume, tears and a tattered reputation. Jesus points out that the issue is not how much is forgiven, but who realizes they need forgiveness.

The Pharisee was the last to recognize who Jesus truly was and the depth of his own sin. This sinful woman recognized both first.

## *Reflections on the Weeping Sinner*

1. What do you think was the woman's plan when she went to Simon's house?

2. What are some strengths we could learn from this sinner?

**Think of the Weeping Sinner when:**

You feel overwhelmed.

You need to find peace.

You need courage to admit your weakness

*Jesus devoted time to teaching and training His disciples, while also engaging with skeptics and those who demanded signs. Large crowds often gathered wherever He went. When His mother Mary and His brothers came to see Him in Capernaum, Jesus used the moment to make a point about spiritual relationships. He declared that family is not defined by blood alone, but by obedience to God: "Those who hear the word of God and do it" are family (Luke 8:21; Mark 3:31–35; Matthew 12:46–50).*

# The Toucher

*Mark 5:21-43; Matthew 9:18-26; Luke 8:40-48*

While Jesus was at the Sea of Galilee, Jairus, a synagogue official, approached and fell at His feet, pleading for help, his young daughter was dying. Jesus went with the man and, a large crowd followed closely, possibly hoping to witness a miracle.

In the crowd was a woman who had suffered from a continuous flow of blood for twelve years. She had spent all her resources seeking help from physicians and remedies, yet her condition only worsened. According to Jewish law, such bleeding rendered her ceremonially unclean, isolating her from others, as anyone who touched her would also become unclean (Ilan, 1996, p. 101).

Despite her suffering and isolation, the woman had been following Jesus and believed that simply touching His cloak would heal her. With faith and desperation, she reached out, and immediately, she felt her body mend. The bleeding stopped.

Jesus, sensing a change, stopped and asked who had touched Him. The woman came forward, trembling, and fell at His feet. She confessed everything.

Rather than rebuking her, Jesus calls her 'Daughter', a term of tenderness. He affirms her faith, assures her of her healing, and sends her away in peace.

Jesus consistently heals those with a chronic illness: the lepers, the paralyzed, the blind, the bent, the withered, the deaf, the mute, etc. He restores the lives of those who were limited. He changes them to a position of service.

## *Reflections on The Toucher*

1. What are some of the limitations that chronic illness brings?

2. When Jesus turns and confronts the woman, the crowd probably goes silent. What strength did the woman use to answer Jesus?

3. What are the woman's strengths?

**Think of the Toucher when**:

You need peace.

You are chronically ill physically or spiritually

You are scared but need to tell the truth.

*Jesus continues to heal the blind, the mute and to teach. He sends out the twelve in pairs to also teach and heal (Matthew 11:1; Mark 6:6-13; Luke 9:1-6).*

*At this point, John the Baptist had been imprisoned by Herod Antipas after publicly condemning his relationship with Herodias. They would have been in the area of Galilee, Herod's territory. It's helpful to review a portion of the Herodian family tree.*

*Herod the Great, known for his paranoia and brutality, had lots of wives and numerous children—many of whom were half-siblings. He executed three of his sons and one wife out of fear they were plotting against him. He had trust issues. The Herodian dynasty is notoriously confusing due to repeated names across generations and intermarriages within the family.*

Four sons of Herod the Great are relevant in this discussion: Aristobulus IV, Herod II (also known as Philip), Herod Antipas, and Philip II the Tetrarch. All were half-brothers.

1. Aristobulus IV married Berenice, Herod the Great's niece. Although Aristobulus was later executed by his father, he left behind a son, Herod Agrippa I, and a daughter, Herodias.
    a. Herod Agrippa I, rose to power through political skill, eventually ruling much of his grandfather's former territory. He is likely the Herod who died in Acts 12:20–23 around 44 CE. His children included Herod Agrippa II and daughters Berenice, Mariamne, and Drusilla.
    b. Herodias was the daughter of Aristobulus and Berenice and granddaughter of Herod the Great. Herodias is included in the next discussion.
2. Herod II (Philip) was apparently disinherited by Herod the Great (although at one time he was a chosen heir) and lived in Rome as a private citizen, without any political influence. He had married Herodias, his niece. Herodias and Herod II had a daughter named Salome (according to Josephus, Antiquities of the Jews 18).
3. Herod Antipas, ruler of Galilee and Perea, was married to a Nabatean princess. During a visit to Rome, he began an affair with Herodias, the wife of his half-brother, Herod II. Both Antipas and Herodias divorce their spouses and marry, igniting a public scandal. The insult to the Nabatean royal family led to a military conflict with Nabataea, a kingdom spanning parts of modern-day Jordan, southern Syria, and northwestern Saudi Arabia.
    a. He lost a significant battle around 36 CE, which according to Josephus (Antiquities 18.5.1) some viewed as punishment for his execution of John.
4. Philip II the Tetrarch ruled Batanea and surrounding regions in modern Syria. He eventually married his niece, Salome, Herod II and Herodias's daughter – the dancer for Herod Antipas.

# *Herodias and Salome*

Mark 6:14-29, Matthew 14:3-12

John the Baptist publicly condemned Herod Antipas for marrying his sister-in-law and other wrongdoings (Luke 3:19). In response, Antipas had John imprisoned. Despite his criticism Herod Antipas held a certain respect for John, recognizing him as a righteous and holy man. He kept John safe in custody and even listened to him with interest and admiration (Mark 6:20).

Herodias probably knew that Antipas had an affinity toward John. Herod would meet with him and listen to his call for repentance. She nursed her resentment toward John, possibly threatened that Herod would follow John's advice and dissolve their marriage. Herodias was seeking a chance to have him killed (Mark 6:19). That opportunity came during Herod Antipas's birthday celebration. As part of the entertainment, Herodias's daughter, Salome, performed a dance that captivated both Herod and his guests. Pleased and probably drinking, Herod made a grand gesture: offering to grant her anything she desired, up to half of his kingdom (Mark 6:21–23). While not literally 'half his kingdom' it was a grand, public offer to Salome.

Salome, with an 'open-ended debit card' goes to her mother and asks for advice. "What shall I ask for?" (Mark 6:24). Herodias's answer was swift and calculated. She instructs her daughter to ask for the head of John the Baptist, immediately.

Salome returns and makes the macabre request. The urgency and specificity of the demand suggest that Herodias had planned it in advance. Though distressed, Herod Antipas honored his vow out of pride and fear of losing face in front of his guests. John was beheaded in prison, and his severed head was brought to Salome on a platter, who gave it to her mother.

The gruesome scene has inspired many dramatic works of art throughout the centuries, capturing the brutality and tragedy of that moment.

## *Reflections on Herodias and Salome*

1. What seems to have motivated Herodias in her actions toward John the Baptist and her marriage decisions?

2. Was Salome a pawn in Herodias's scheme or did she have a choice?

3. What are Herodias's strengths?

4. Herodias was a murderer. While we don't act to the extent she did, what are her weaknesses that we also struggle to control?

5. Ultimately, Salome's actions define her character. What are her strengths and weaknesses?

**Think of Herodias when:**

You hold a grudge.

It is difficult to repent.

Others may be involved in your decisions.

**Think of Salome when:**

You use your opportunity to harm others.

Obedience to others requires sin.

*After the twelve return from their mission of teaching and healing, Jesus miraculously feeds thousands and then sends His disciples ahead by boat. That evening, He walks across the Sea of Galilee to rejoin them. Shortly afterward, Jesus withdraws from Jewish regions and travels to the coast in Phoenicia on the Mediterranean.*

# Canaanite Woman

*Matthew 15:21-28, Mark 7:24-30*

Mark records that Jesus entered the area of Tyre and Sidon quietly, hoping to remain unnoticed. Jesus and his disciples traveled 50-60 miles from Capernaum to 'get away'. It appears He was seeking a break, away from the crowds in Judah. It would have been a 2-3 day walk to visit the coast, yet word of His presence quickly spread.

The town of Zarephath is in the area and may sound familiar. It is the same town where the prophet Elijah stayed during the great drought. (Luke 4:26) There, Elijah lived with a widow and her son, miraculously providing food for them. When the boy died, Elijah prayed, and God raised him from the dead (1 Kings 17:8–24). Once again, Jesus was walking in the footsteps of the prophets who came before Him.

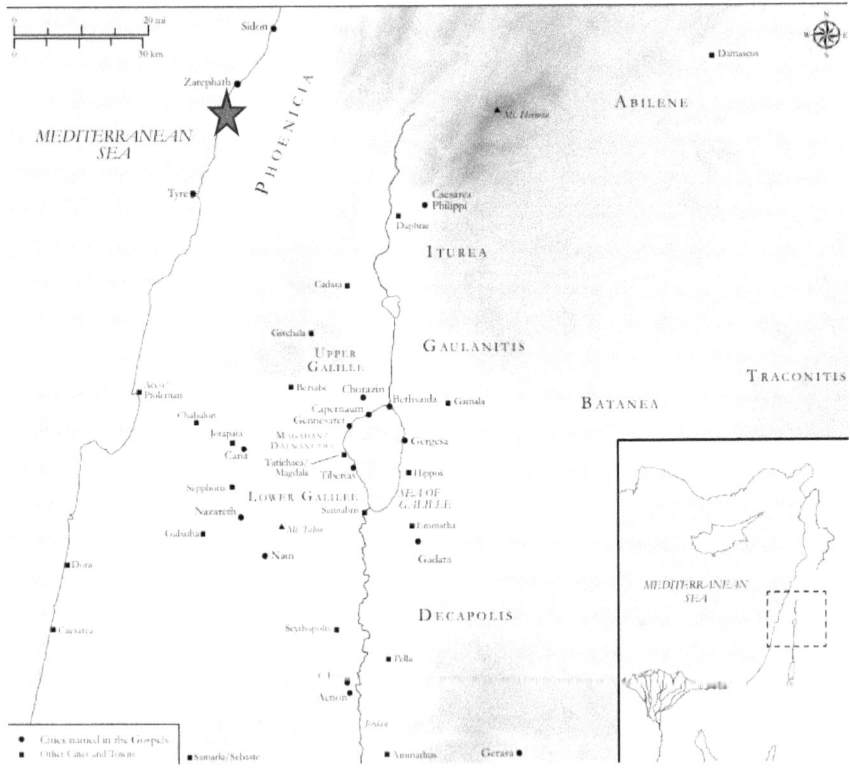

In that region lived a Phoenician woman whose young daughter was tormented by an unclean spirit. Upon hearing about Jesus in the area, she found Him, then fell at His feet, pleading for her child's healing. Jesus explained that His mission was first to the house of Israel, using the image of a family table:

*'It is not right to take the children's bread and throw it to the dogs' (Mark 7:27).*

Undeterred, the Gentile woman didn't dispute priority, and accepted the comparison to a dog with humility, appealing for mercy,

*'Even the dogs under the table eat the children's crumbs.' (Mark 7:28)*

Her hope, belief, and persistence moved Jesus. He told her to return home, assuring her that the demon had left her daughter. She didn't argue or insist He come with her. Like the faith of the centurion, she simply believed Jesus and returned home, finding her daughter exactly as He had said (Matthew 8:5-13).

This Canaanite woman could teach a master class in negotiations! First, set a clear goal: her daughter healed.

She began with a disadvantaged starting point, as an outsider. However, she was respectful and persistent. She knows Jesus as the "Son of David" and accepts the limitation that He was sent to Isarel's 'lost sheep' first. But this mother recognized that Jesus's comments did not eliminate action. Jesus is the bread of life, and even a crumb was enough. She worked with His metaphor of 'children and dogs' to reframe it: 'Even dogs...' She did not demand a Jew visit a Gentile home or require a touch but made a 'low cost' request. Just say the word. Finally, she trusted that when Jesus said her daughter was healed it was done. Ultimately, this Canaanite mother is an example of seek and you will find - She sought Jesus and found healing.

## *Reflections on the Canaanite Woman*

1. If the Canaanite had been insulted by Jesus's analogy, what would she have done?

    a. Do we every get insulted and walk away from an opportunity to glorify God?

2. This Canaanite and the centurion both had faith that Jesus's words alone would 'make it so'. Were there other commonalities?

3. What are some negotiation skills the Phoenician used?

4. What are the strengths of this Phoenician woman?

**Think of the Canaanite Woman when:**

You are an outsider needing help.

Your pride keeps you from asking for and receiving help.

You need to negotiate

# *Mary Magdalene, Joanna, Susanna and others*

*Luke 8: 1-3*

As Jesus continued His ministry, healing, feeding thousands, and teaching, He and His disciples traveled through Galilee, Magdala (Mark 8:10), Bethsaida (Mark 8:22), and Caesarea Philippi (Matthew 16:13). Luke notes that several women were part of His traveling group. Some had been healed of evil spirits and sicknesses. Among them were Mary Magdalene, from whom Jesus cast out seven demons; Joanna, the wife of Chuza, Herod's steward (likely Herod Antipas, ruler over Galilee and Perea); Susanna; and many others who offered practical and financial support (Luke 8:1–3).

Where did these women gain the resources to support Jesus's ministry? Although Jewish customs and Roman law limited women's independence, they still had avenues for income. The daughters of Zelophehad (Numbers 27:1–9; 36:1–13; Joshua 17:3–4) established the legal right for daughters to inherit property in certain cases. Women could also profit from their own handiwork or that of their servants. Spinning wool or flax into thread, weaving fabric, or making clothing were potential sources of income (Ilan, 1996, page 186).

Historical records suggest women worked as shopkeepers, midwives, wet nurses, herbalists, professional mourners, hairdressers, and innkeepers (though innkeeping was considered low-status) (Ilan, 1996, 186–188). Priscilla, for instance, worked alongside her husband and Paul as a tentmaker (Acts 18:3). However, women were not allowed in schools to study scriptures or recognized as rabbinic disciples. In contrast, Jesus includes women in his disciples. They would have learned from Him directly. For example, the angels at the tomb remind the women how he had taught them that the Son of man must die and would rise again (Luke 24:4-8). Jesus included the women in his teachings and with his disciples.

Some of the women who followed Jesus may have had businesses or households that continued running in their absence. Interestingly, the Babylonian Talmud interprets the name "Magdalene" as referring to a hairdresser (Ilan, 1996,188–189). Luke's account highlights not only the spiritual devotion of these women, but also their practical contributions: making ministry possible through their faithful support.

Growing up I assumed Jesus's disciples were mostly the apostles. However, in Luke 10, Jesus send out seventy others, and Acts 1:21–23 notes that when a replacement for Judas was chosen, two men who had been with them from the beginning were suggested. This indicates that the group of disciples was broader than just the apostles. In Matthew 20:20–21, the mother of James and John approaches Jesus with a request, indicating a level of familiarity and access that suggests she was part of the traveling group of disciples.

These women that Luke includes are also mentioned by Mark, Matthew, Luke, and John as disciples at the cross. It seems these women recognized Jesus as the Messiah and became part of the disciples he taught. Now, when I read about Jesus teaching parables, explaining generosity, or preparing His disciples for His suffering (Matthew 13:36; Mark 12:43; Mark 9:31), I picture women present among the disciples, listening and learning at Jesus's feet.

## *Reflections on Mary Magdalene, Joanna, Susanna and others*

1. How do you think the women helped during Jesus's work?

2. To leave your home and travel with Jesus would take quite a commitment. What strengths allowed these women to support Jesus in his work?

3. If women were not allowed in the schools and had separate spaces in synagogues and the temple, how would Jesus's inclusion of the women with his disciples challenge norms?

**Think of Jesus's Travel Entourage when:**

You see an exceptional opportunity to make a difference.

You think of Jesus disciples as only male.

*Jesus continued His ministry throughout Galilee before traveling to Jerusalem for the Feast of Tabernacles (also called the Feast of Booths), which took place in late September or early October (John 7:14). While in Jerusalem, reactions to Him were mixed, some questioned whether He might be the Messiah, the religious leaders sought to arrest Him, yet many others came to believe in Him (John 7:26, 30–31).*

# *Adulterer*

*John 8:2-11*

The Jewish leaders were actively looking for ways to discredit and accuse Jesus of wrongdoing. One morning at the end of the Feast of Tabernacles, while Jesus was teaching in the temple, the scribes and Pharisees brought before Him a woman caught in the act of adultery. They placed her in front of the crowd and declared her guilt, asking Jesus to pronounce judgment. You can feel the trap being set. Moses's law commanded that such a woman be stoned (Leviticus 20:10; Deuteronomy 22:21–24). Would Jesus authorize her execution or contradict Moses?

Jesus didn't respond with a debate. He didn't question where the man was, since adultery involved two people, nor did He ask whether due process had been followed. Jesus didn't judge as we judge. Instead, He bent down and wrote on the ground. Then He stood and said, 'Let the one among you who is without sin cast the first stone.' After speaking, He returned to writing on the ground.

One by one, beginning with the oldest, the accusers quietly slipped away. They knew their own guilt. Eventually, only Jesus and the woman remained in the courtyard.

The religious leaders were using the law as a weapon. Jesus uses it as a mirror. "And why behold thou the mote that is in thy brother's eye, but consider not the beam that is in thine own eye?" Matthew 7:3. For this woman, He puts his teaching into practice. Jesus asks the religious leaders to address her sin, once they have cleared their own sin. Individually they realized they did not have the right to condemn her.

It had likely been the most terrifying day of her life. What may have begun in sinful passion ended in fear, exposure, and public shame. How tempting would it be to leave? Duck and run? Yet, she didn't run when the crowd dispersed. She stayed, perhaps waiting to hear Jesus's verdict.

Jesus asked her, 'Woman, where are they? Has no one condemned you?' (John 8:10). She respectfully replied, 'No one, Lord.'

Jesus chooses not condemn her with the condition that she does not sin any more. He offered mercy with the opportunity to change. She had another chance. We're not told what became of her, but we can hope she became a disciple of Jesus.

Note: John 8:1-11 is not in the three oldest manuscripts of John.

## *Reflections on the Adulterer*

1. Why do you think she stayed when all her accusers had left? Why not run?

2. There was a show that put minor offenders in with criminals, so the minor offenders would be 'scared straight'. A moment of clarity where the outcome of your choices becomes undeniable. We don't know the outcome, but the adulterer had an experience that would be difficult to forget. What would it take for you to be 'scared straight' from your secret sin?

**Think of the adulterer when:**

You want to run instead of facing the consequences

You struggle with a secret sin.

# *Blind Man's Mother*

*John 9:1-41*

On the Sabbath in Jerusalem, Jesus encounters a man who was blind from birth. His disciples question why he was born blind. Frequently we want to cast blame when people suffer. Jesus dismisses the idea that sin created the blindness. He tells His disciples that the man's condition exists so that the works of God might be displayed. Jesus then makes mud with His saliva, applies it to the man's eyes, and instructs him to wash in the Pool of Siloam. The man obeys and returns with his sight restored.

When the healed man shares what happened, some of the Pharisees dismiss the miracle, insisting that Jesus could not be from God since He healed on the Sabbath[2]. Unconvinced that the man had truly been blind, they summon his parents for questioning. His mother and father confirm that he is their son and that he was born blind, but they avoid answering how he was healed and who healed him. Fearing pressures from the leaders, they defer all other questions to their grown son.

The leaders had spread threats that anyone who confessed Jesus as the Messiah would be expelled from the synagogue. Excommunication involved a formal process, beginning with a specific charge and legal hearing, neither of which had yet occurred, but the threat was enough to cause fear and keep some people from talking about Jesus.

When questioned again, the healed man boldly challenges the religious leaders, saying that God hears those who fear Him and do His will. Offended, they cast him out.

Later, Jesus finds him and asks, "Do you believe in the Son of Man?" This man's faith has grown in stages. At first, he said the 'man called Jesus' (v.11), next 'He is a prophet' (v.17), then 'if this man were not from God' (v.33) and finally he responds in faith,

---

[2] The Gospels record seven miracles Jesus performed on the Sabbath. Mark 1:21-28, Mark 1:29-31, Mark 3:1-6, Luke 13:10-17, Luke 14:1-6, John 5:1-18, John 9:1-41.

'Lord, I believe' (v.38) and worships Jesus. The blind man sees physically and over time sees the spiritual truth of Jesus as well.

We don't know if the Blind Man's parents ever acknowledged Jesus as the one who gives sight.

## *Reflections on Blind Man's Mother*

All the responses are from both parents,

1. If someone healed your child from a debilitating illness, what would keep you from telling everyone the good news?

2. What weakness do you think the mother of the Blind Man struggles?

**Think of the Blind Man's Mother when:**

You are afraid to tell others about Jesus.

*After sending out seventy followers to teach and heal (Luke 10:1–24), Jesus continued His journey, teaching along the way. He eventually stopped in the village of Bethany.*

# *Mary and Martha Part 1*

*Luke 10:38-42*

Mary, Martha, and Lazarus were close friends of Jesus who lived in the village of Bethany. The Gospels record at least two occasions when Jesus visited their home, though He likely spent more time with the family than what is mentioned, as they seem to have a close relationship[3].

On one of these visits, Martha warmly welcomed Jesus into her home. While He spoke with those gathered, Martha busied herself with the responsibilities of hospitality, preparing and serving, ensuring everything was just right. Meanwhile, her sister Mary sat at Jesus' feet, as a student to a Rabbi, listening intently to His words instead of helping with the tasks. Women were not allowed to learn scriptures formally, so this was a rare opportunity to be taught.

Martha, clearly feeling frustrated with the work needing to be done, turned to Jesus for support. She was exasperated that Mary wasn't helping and asked Jesus to intervene. Her request suggests a level of familiarity and friendship with Him. Her question is not an approach you take with a stranger.

I can almost imagine Jesus smiling gently as He replied,

> *"Martha, Martha, you are worried and distracted by many things; but only one thing is necessary; for Mary has chosen the good part, which shall not be taken away from her." Luke 10:41b-42.*

Jesus affirmed that while Martha's efforts were well-intentioned, Mary had chosen something greater: spiritual nourishment. He would not take that away from her.

A woman listening with the men was not something allowed in schools, synagogues or in the Temple. Jesus did not limit his teachings to men. Jesus defends Mary's ability to learn alongside men. Women such as Mary were included, protected and defended to learn and be disciples.

We aren't told how Martha responded at that moment, but we do know that her faith didn't waver. Hopefully, Martha stopped and

---

[3] Their third interaction with Jesus was at Simon the Leper's house.

joined Mary. In a later encounter, she confesses her belief in Jesus as the Messiah. Martha had deep faith but showed it differently than Mary. It is good to note that Jesus didn't condemn Martha's efforts but defended Mary's choice. Later when Martha is with Jesus is at Simon's home, she is once again serving, faithful in her own way.

## *Reflections on Mary and Martha Part 1*

1. Did Martha need the same spiritual food as Mary?

2. What does Jesus's defense of Mary's right to learn alongside the male disciples, rather than being separated or confined to serving, reveal about His view of women's roles?

3. It is easy to choose sides, Mary or Martha. What are the joys of being "a Mary?" Is there also pleasure in serving like Martha?

**Think of Martha when:**

You are too busy to focus on spiritual food.

We expect others to need the same spiritual food we want.

**Think of Mary sister of Martha when:**

You need spiritual food from Jesus.

*Jesus continues to teach on prayer, the importance of persistence, and addressing false accusations, including the claim that His power came from Beelzebub.*

# *Blessing Woman*

Luke 11:27-28

As Jesus is teaching, a woman in the crowd calls out a blessing for His mother, expressing admiration for the one who bore and nursed Him. Her words suggest that she attributes Jesus's wisdom and authority to His family.

Jesus does not rebuke her directly or speak negatively about His family, but He redirects the focus. Instead of emphasizing biological ties, He declares that true blessing belongs to those who hear the word of God and put it into practice.

This is very similar when Mary and His brothers visited at Capernaum and when told they were outside, Jesus responds his mother, brothers and sisters are those that do the will of His Father (Luke 8:21; Mark 3:31–35; Matthew 12:46–50).

The Blessing Woman meant well. Most of us enjoy hearing compliments to our family. But we should not forget the value of our spiritual family.

## *Reflections on Blessing Woman*

1. Does it matter what we bless?

2. What is the weakness of the Blessing woman?

**Think of the Blessing Woman when:**

You need a reminder to cherish your spiritual family.

# *Bent Woman*

*Luke 13:10-17*

As Jesus traveled through towns and villages on His way to Jerusalem, He taught on many topics: warning against hypocrisy, greed, and anxiety, and urging His listeners to stay watchful and prepared for the Master's return. On one Sabbath, He is teaching at a synagogue and noticed a woman. For eighteen years, the woman had been bent over, unable to stand up straight. When Jesus saw her, He called out:

*"Woman, thou art loosed from thine infirmity." Luke 13:12b*

She responded to His voice and came forward. Jesus laid His hands on her, and for the first time in nearly two decades, she stood upright. (I can't help but smile imagining how her clothes, shaped to fit her bent frame, now hung awkwardly on her healed body, but she wouldn't care in the least.)

Her immediate response was to glorify God. She didn't question who Jesus was or whether healing should take place on the Sabbath. She recognized that God had been glorified.

But not everyone rejoiced. The synagogue leader objected, insisting that healing should be done on the other six days of the week, not the Sabbath. Jesus exposes the hypocrisy of such thinking: they would untie and lead their animals to water on the Sabbath, yet object to a woman being set free from suffering?

Despite her discomfort, the woman had come to the synagogue on the Sabbath. Scripture does not suggest that she was seeking Jesus or had come to be healed. She would go to the synagogue to worship Jehovah. Jesus found her and took pity.

Jesus called her a "daughter of Abraham," a title that likely recognized her as a faithful Jew, or perhaps as a woman whose faith resembled Abraham's own. Either way, she received God's mercy and instantly glorified God.

Frequently Jesus's teaching or actions have another layer of teaching. In this healing, Jesus calls out Satan as the aggressor holding this "daughter of Abraham" in bondage. Jesus's actions show those at the synagogue that He is the strong man who will release those in bondage to Satan (Luke 11:22). It was particularly fitting that the woman's 'release from bondage' was on the sabbath. The sabbath rest was a day to remember when Jehovah liberated the Hebrews out of Egyptian bondage (Deuteronomy 5:15). Jesus teaches and demonstrates that He is the Messiah bringing salvation, releasing us from the bondage of sin.

## *Reflections on Bent Woman*

1. How might living with a long-term illness affect someone's relationship with God?

2. 'Luck is what happens when preparation meets opportunity', is a saying attributed to Seneca, a Roman philosopher. This reflects the idea that being in the right place, doing the right thing, positions someone when the moment arrives. Did the woman 'get lucky' or does her healing reflect her faithful presence in worship?

3. What would you suggest are the Bent woman's strengths?

**Think of the Bent Woman when:**

It is difficult to worship God.

Your chronic aches and pains keep you from God.

Others elevate law above helping others.

*Luke and John record Jesus's teachings and travels through Perea and the area around Jerusalem (Luke 13–17; John 10). During this time, He taught about the kingdom of God, mourned over Jerusalem, exposed hypocrisy, and shared many parables. The time is close to the Passover and the end of Jesus's ministry (John 11:55).*

# *Mary and Martha Part 2*

*John 11:1-44*

Lazarus fell seriously ill, and his sisters, Mary and Martha, sent a message to Jesus: their brother was sick. Yet Jesus did not rush to his side. Though He loved the family, He delayed His departure. His disciples were concerned about returning to Judea, especially near Jerusalem. Some of the Jewish leaders had recently threatened Jesus, and hostility toward Him was growing (John 10:31, 39; 11:8, 16). After waiting two days, Jesus told His disciples it was time to go. By the time they arrived in Bethany, Lazarus had been dead and buried for four days. Some Jewish traditions held that the soul lingered near the body for three days before departure. The four days removes any suggestion that Lazarus was not dead.

When word reached Martha that Jesus was approaching, she left the house, leaving behind the mourners, to meet Him. Her first words were filled with both accusation and faith:

> *"Lord, if You had been here, my brother would not have died. Even now I know that whatever You ask of God, God will give You." John 11:21b-22.*

Jesus assured her, "Your brother will rise again." Martha replied with confidence in a future resurrection, saying she believed Lazarus would rise on the last day. Martha held a belief that there is eternal life. But Jesus declares:

> *"I am the resurrection and the life; the one who believes in Me will live, even if he dies, and everyone who lives and believes in Me will never die. Do you believe this?" John 11:25-26.*

Martha then makes her confession of faith:

> *"I have believed that thou art the Christ, the Son of God, even he that cometh into the world." John 11:27b*

After waiting, Martha's faith grows from belief in doctrine of the resurrection to trust in Jesus, the Son of God.

Martha goes to quietly bring Mary to Jesus. However, she is followed by friends who had come to comfort them. When Mary reaches Jesus, she falls at His feet and echoes her sister's words:

*"Lord, if You had been here, my brother would not have died." John 11:32b.*

Martha and Mary voiced a concern many wrestle with: *If God can prevent suffering, why doesn't He?* Their words carried both sorrow, hope, and perhaps disappointment that Jesus didn't do all he could to help. Yet Martha and Mary continued to recognized Jesus' divine authority. They didn't know at the time, but Jesus knew he was going to bring Lazarus back. They would not need to wait long before Lazarus would be with them again.

However, Jesus feels their grief and weeps with them. He cries for their pain and with tears of God over sin and death's intrusion into His creation.

At the tomb, Jesus asked for the stone to be rolled away. Ever practical, Martha objected, warning that there would be a strong odor. But Jesus gently reminded her,

*"Did I not say to you that if you believe, you will see the glory of God?" John 11:40.*

Then, in the presence of the crowd, Jesus prayed aloud, not for His own sake, but so those around Him would know the miracle came from the Father. Afterward, He commands for Lazarus to come out of the grave. To everyone's astonishment, Lazarus emerged, alive and still wrapped in burial cloths. Jesus told the people there to unbind him and let him go. Jesus frees us from death, but we are expected to participate in the liberation. In that moment, sorrow turned to joy as Lazarus was restored to life and reunited with the living.

This was a sign that revealed hearts. Many who had come to Mary and Martha believed and found faith, but some gathered to plot his demise (John 11:45-46). The miracle of Lazarus's resurrection from the grave accelerated the chief priests and the council's plans to put Jesus in the grave (John 11:53).

## *Reflections on Mary and Martha Part 2*

1. Why would Martha, Mary and the others expect Jesus to keep Lazarus from dying?

2. From Martha's declaration in John 11:27 what do we know about her developing faith?

**Think of Mary and Martha when:**

God doesn't answer in your time frame.

God is the only one who can help.

*After raising Lazarus from the dead Jesus goes to the Jericho area, heals Bartimaeus, eats with Zacchaeus, and continues to teach.*

# *Mother of James and John*

*Matthew 20:20-28*

Women continued to travel with Jesus and the disciples, including the mother of James and John, Mrs. Zebedee. At one point, she approaches Jesus, bows before Him, and asks that her sons be granted the honor of sitting at His right and left in His kingdom, positions of highest authority next to Jesus Himself. Her sons are present, and Jesus responds that they do not understand what they are asking. He then explains that such positions are not His to grant but are determined by God. In Mark 10:35–40, the same request is recorded, but Mark does not mention the request was initiated by Salome, possibly the name of James and John's mother.

The request by James and John's mom gives us insight into the understanding of many of Jesus's disciples: This was an earthly kingdom with a king and officers. She approached as a petitioner would to a king by kneeling and requesting a favor. The right-hand person might be the Praetorian Prefect, head of security, or prime minister. The left-hand might be generals and trusted heirs. Salome was asking that Jesus give her sons titles and power to rule.

Jesus agrees that they will share in His cup of suffering. Then, He follows with the leadership system in His kingdom: the great will be servants. He explains that his life will be laid down as the redemption price for many.

Not the answer James and John's mom expected. But it doesn't change her support of Jesus. We will see her again at Jesus's cross with the other women and John. She will see criminals on Jesus's right and left (Matthew 27:38). Maybe a sign that her request was not what she really wanted.

While John lives a long and productive life for Christ, her son James will be killed by Herod Agrippa in about 10 years (Acts 12:1-2).

## *Reflections on the Mother of James and John*

1. What characteristic would Salome have to make this request of Jesus?

2. Why would Salome continue to support Jesus even as her request is denied?

**Think of the Mother of James and John:**

You put physical power before spiritual.

*Jesus continues to teach and heals two blind men.*

# *Mary and Martha Part 3*

*Mark 14:3-9, Matthew 26:6-13, John 12:1-8*

On the Saturday before Passover, Jesus arrives in Bethany. Mark, Matthew and John offer complementary details about the dinner that evening, forming a more complete picture when combined. According to Mark and Matthew, the meal takes place at the home of Simon the Leper. John notes that Martha is serving, and Lazarus, whom Jesus had raised from the dead, is among those reclining at the table with Him.

During the meal, Mary takes a jar of pure nard (spikenard), a fragrant and costly perfume imported from the mountains of India or the Himalayas, valued at nearly a year's wages, and begins to anoint Jesus. Mark records that she anoints His head, intentionally breaking the jar, while John adds that she also anoints His feet and wipes them with her hair, filling the house with the fragrance. It is difficult to fathom the relationship and the value Mary, Martha and Lazarus had for Jesus.

Kings were anointed on the head and bodies were anointed for burial. Mary's actions acknowledged His authority and her understanding of His teaching that He would die. By breaking the jar, Mary removed any chance of any of the ointment being held back. It would all be poured out. We don't know what Mary was thinking, but as the disciples prepared for a kingdom, Mary's actions were preparing Jesus for his sacrifice.

Judas Iscariot and others object, protesting that the perfume could have been sold and the money given to the poor. But Jesus defends Mary. He says she has anointed Him in preparation for His burial. "She has done what she could," He affirms, and declares that her act of love will be remembered wherever the gospel is preached.

This is the second time Jesus has defended Mary. While some measure value on usefulness for their goals, Mary saw the value in Jesus.

## *Reflections on Mary and Martha Part 3*

1. Are you surprised that Martha is serving?

2. Jesus prophesies that Mary would be remember for her work. Did that happen?

3. Jesus defends Mary again. What was Mary doing this time that Jesus defended (Luke 10:39, John 12:3)?

Our first interaction with Mary and Martha focuses on their exchange with Jesus. The second shared Martha's faith at the raising of Lazarus. The last story showed Mary's understanding of Jesus's mission. Over the three events of Mary and Martha in Part 1, 2 and 3 consider:

4. How would you describe Martha's strengths?

5. What are Mary's strengths?

**Think of Mary and Martha when:**

You want to honor Jesus.

You think your gift to glorify Jesus is generous.

*Over the next few days Jesus triumphantly enters Jerusalem, teaching at the temple and returning to Bethany in the evening. The Pharisees and Sadducees test Him, and His parables point to their hypocrisy. While at the temple Jesus says to beware of the scribes...who like the best seats.. consume widow's houses ..make long pretentious prayers .... Mark 12:38-40, Luke 20:45-47.*

# *Giving Widow*

*Mark 12:41-44, Luke 21:1-4*

After warning the people about the behavior of certain scribes that devour widow's houses (Mark 12: 40), Jesus sits down with his disciples across from the temple treasury. He watches wealthy individuals contribute large sums of money. Then He brings the disciples attention to a poor widow approaching. She placed two small coins into the offering, everything she has to live on. She could have kept one, but she does not. She gives all.

Jesus uses this moment to illustrate an important economic principle: utility. To the wealthy, two small coins are insignificant, virtually worthless. But to the widow, those same two coins hold immense value. In economic terms, their utility is far greater for her than for someone who has abundance. [4]

If we focus only on the monetary value of her gift, it appears inconsequential. Her offering does not change the total wealth of the treasury. But when we consider what she gave in proportion to what she had, her sacrifice becomes profound. Those two coins may have meant the difference between eating or going hungry. They carried immense usefulness, high utility, for her. In contrast, what the rich gave did not affect whether they would eat that evening. The rich would have to give until they were not sure of their next meal to match the widow's generosity.

Perhaps the widow was motivated by faith. The widow showed where she found security. Money was not where she put her trust. She depended on God. Perhaps she had heard David's words in the psalms:

*'I have been young and now I am old, Yet I have not seen the righteous forsaken or his descendants begging for bread.' Psalms 37:25.*

---

[4] See St. Petersburg Paradox, the Bernoulli family, and the concept of utility in economics. This was a concept that took centuries for academics to recognize, that Jesus had taught centuries before.

Jesus presents her as an example of someone who not only believed in her dependence on God but demonstrated it through her actions. God is not impressed by gifts that cost us nothing (David's example in 2 Samuel 24:24).

## *Reflections on the Giving Widow*

1. What does the widow teach us about generosity and dependence on God?

**Think of the Giving Widow when:**

You forget to depend on God.

*Jesus teaches his disciples at the Mount of Olives and talks about the future. Judas begins negotiations with the Pharisees. Jesus and His disciples share a meal, sing a hymn and pray. While Jesus and the disciples were in the Garden Judas brings a group of officers. He identifies Jesus who is then bound and taken to Annas, the High Priest, and is later presented to Caiphas.*

# *Servant woman*

*Mark 14:66, Matthew 26:69- 75, Luke 22: 54-61, John 18: 15-18, 25-27*

There was a servant at the courtyard of the High Priest who recognized Peter as one of Jesus's disciples. At her question, Peter denies he is Jesus's disciple.

Others then question Peter, and he denies being associated with Jesus two additional times.

## *Reflection on the Servant woman*

1. Why would she care if Jesus's disciple was in the courtyard?

*Jesus is taken from Caiaphas to Pilate the Roman Prefect for the area. When Pilate learns Jesus is from Galilee, he sends him to Herod Antipas, who was in Jerusalem for the Passover. Herod returns Jesus to Pilate.*

# *Pilate's Wife*

*Matthew 27:18-19*

Pilate knew Jesus was not guilty, and while he was sitting in his Judgement seat, his wife sent him a message.

> *"See that you have nothing to do with that righteous Man; for last night I suffered greatly in a dream because of Him." Matthew 27:19b.*

Pilate's wife had a troubling dream about Jesus that disturbed her. From her dream, she knew Jesus was blameless. She wrote a note to warn her husband. Jesus was righteous. Do not get involved! Pilate agreed with his wife but yielded to the Jew's demand for Jesus's death, sealing his legacy.

Historical records note that Pilate was later removed from office after violently suppressing a Samaritan uprising (around 36 CE) and sent to Rome for a hearing. However, Emperor Tiberius died before it took place. Tradition varies on his fate: some sources in the Ethiopian Orthodox Tewahedo Church suggest that Pilate and his wife became Christians, while others say he retired. Ultimately, the later lives of both remain uncertain.

Pilate's wife stands out in the Gospel narrative as the only recorded person to speak in Jesus's defense. The last witness testifying to Jesus's innocence. A Gentile who received a message and shared it, trying to keep her husband from his biggest mistake.

## *Reflections on Pilate's wife*

1. Why would Pilate's wife care if her husband ruled against Jesus?

**Think of Pilate's wife when:**

You warn someone, but they don't listen.

# *The Cross: Mary Magdalene, Mary, Mary, Salome, Joanna*

*Mark 15:31-32,39-41, Matthew 27:38, 41-44, 54-56, Luke 23:33-33,49, John 19:25-27*

At the close of the first day of Unleavened Bread, during the Passover, Jesus and His disciples shared a final meal together. They ate, talked, prayed, and sang a hymn before going out to the Mount of Olives. There, Jesus warned them that they would soon abandon Him:

*'I will strike the shepherd, and the sheep of the flock will be scattered.' Zechariah 13:7.*

Yet He also reassured them that He would meet them again in Galilee (*Mark 14:22–28; Matthew 26:26–32*).

Jesus is taken by the soldiers from the garden to Annas, the High Priest, and is later presented to Caiphas. They then took Him to Pilate, who sends him to Herod. After multiple beatings he is taken to Golgotha, nailed to a cross and left to die.

The gospels share varying perspectives at the cross. A summary of those recorded in the area when Jesus was hung on a cross to die include:

| At the Cross | Scripture |
|---|---|
| **Roman centurion and soldiers** | Matt 27:54, Mark 15:39, Luke 23:36, 47 |
| **Two criminals (thieves)** | Matt 27:38,44, Luke 23:33 |
| **Chief priests, scribes, elders, and others mocking** | Matt 27:41–43, Mark 15:31–32, Luke 23:35 |
| **Acquaintances & women followers from Galilee** | Luke 23:49 |
| **John the apostle** | John 19:26–27 |
| **Mary Magdalene** | Matt 27:56, Mark 15:40-41, John 19:25 |
| **Mary the mother of James and Joses**** | Matt 27:56, Mark 15:40 |
| **Mary the wife of Clopas**** | John 19:25 |

| | |
|---|---|
| **Mary the mother of Jesus** | John 19:25 |
| **Mary's sister*** | John 19:25 |
| **Salome*** | Mark 15:40 |
| **The mother of the sons of Zebedee*** | Matt 27:56 |
| **Many other women (Galilee)** | Matt 27:55, Mark 15:41; Luke 23:49 |

Some scholars believe that *"the mother of the sons of Zebedee*,"* *"Salome*,"* and *"Mary's sister*"* may all refer to the same woman, described differently by each Gospel writer. Likewise, *"Mary, the mother of James the Less and Joses**"* may be the same person as *"Mary, the wife of Clopas**."* Several other women from Galilee also remained nearby, watching from a distance. Luke mentions Joanna and Susanna was also among the women who had followed Jesus and supported His ministry, and may have been part of the women from Galilee (*Luke 8:1–3*).

Aside from John, none of the other apostles are recorded as remaining with Jesus during His suffering and death. Yet the women stayed: Mary Magdalene, Mary the wife of Clopas, Salome, and women who had followed Him from Galilee, supported His ministry, and now stood near the cross.

Among those at the cross was Mary, the mother of Jesus. Her story is discussed separately.

We can only imagine how those at the cross felt, the grief of watching the One they loved suffer and die, the horror of the cross, the helplessness of standing nearby, unable to intervene. Their faithfulness didn't make it easier; it simply meant they stayed. Within sight. Within hearing. They were the last. They didn't realize yet that their sorrow was not the end of the story.

After Jesus' death, Joseph of Arimathea, a member of the council who had not consented to their decision, went boldly to Pilate to request Jesus' body. Together with Nicodemus, he wrapped the body in a linen shroud and placed it in a nearby tomb.

This act of devotion was risky; it made them ceremonially unclean during Passover and likely brought rejection from other Pharisees.

Meanwhile, Mary Magdalene, Mary the mother of Joses, and several other women from Galilee followed Joseph and Nicodemus, carefully observing where Jesus was laid. How did they feel as they saw His body placed in the tomb? We don't read about their thoughts or emotions, but we know their actions. They returned home to prepare additional spices and ointments and then rested on the Sabbath (*Mark 15:47; Matthew 27:57–61; Luke 23:55–56; John 19:38–42*).

It must have been a long, heartbreaking time. The women from Galilee were away from home. Their hope was buried, yet their love remained steadfast. These women showed up, did what they could, then went back and arranged to do more: preparing, waiting, and resting. Unaware that the dawn of resurrection was drawing near.

## *Reflections on Women at the Cross*

1. Why would these women choose to be with Jesus throughout his suffering and death?

2. Why would others choose to avoid watching Jesus die?

3. Once Jesus was in the tomb, what did the women do?

4. What are some ways to deal with grief?

**Think of the Women at the cross when:**

Someone you love is dying.

Hope is difficult to find.

You are coping with grief.

# *Mary, mother of Jesus at the Cross Part 3*

*John 19:26-27; Acts 1:14*

Mary, likely a widow and in her late forties or fifties, stood near the cross with her sister and two "other Marys" as Jesus endured crucifixion. Perhaps she remembered the words of Simeon spoken decades earlier at the temple:

> *'and a sword shall pierce through thine own soul; that thoughts out of many hearts may be revealed.' Luke 2:35*

Mary is suffering, and in those agonizing hours, Jesus unites His mother, Mary, with John:

> *"Woman, behold your son!... Behold your mother."*
> *John 19:26–27*

At first glance, Jesus's words from the cross may seem like a simple act of ensuring His mother's care. In first-century Jewish culture, the duty of caring for a widowed mother rightly belonged to her son. Mary had four other sons and daughters, and Scripture records that her sons had accompanied her on several occasions, traveling together to Capernaum and later seeking Jesus while He taught (Mark 6:3, John 2:12; Matthew 12:46–50). Clearly, Mary was not abandoned or neglected by her family.

Yet Jesus's decision to entrust Mary to John instead of her other sons seems significant. At the time, His brothers were not believers (John 7:5). In the book of Acts, however, after the ascension, the apostles gather for prayer with "the women, and Mary the mother of Jesus, and His brothers" (Acts 1:14). The very men who had once doubted now stood among the faithful. James, one of Mary's sons, would go on to become a prominent leader in the Jerusalem church and probable writer of the book of James (Galatians 1:18–19; 2:9,12).

Therefore, when Jesus asked Mary to live with John, He was, in essence, removing her from her sons, daughters, and grandchildren to dwell with John, the disciple He loved. If Mary's physical care was not in jeopardy, then perhaps this act was not primarily for Mary's benefit, but for John's.

Consider John's character during Jesus's ministry. When a Samaritan village refused to receive them, John and his brother James wanted to call down fire from heaven to destroy it (Luke 9:51–55). Their fiery temperament earned them the nickname "Sons of Thunder" (Mark 3:17). On the road to Jerusalem, John, along with James and their mother, boldly asked Jesus for seats of honor at His right and left hand in the coming kingdom (Mark 10:35–37; Matthew 20:20–23). This pursuit of status stirred resentment among the other disciples. John was passionate and loyal, but also ambitious and quick-tempered.

Yet at the cross, it is John and the women who remain. In the hour of Jesus's suffering, his loyalty eclipses his pride. When Jesus entrusts Mary to John's care, the "Son of Thunder" receives not only a responsibility, but a refining grace. From that day forward, John took Mary into his home (John 19:27). He apparently never married but served faithfully for the rest of his life.

In later years, John's writings reflect a man transformed, a disciple whose thunderous spirit had been tempered by love. One can imagine the quiet influence of Mary within his home: her steadfast faith, her humility, her deep compassion. Mary, who had been with Jesus longer than any other on earth, would have softened his impulsive zeal and deepened his understanding of love, mercy, and obedience. In giving Mary to John, Jesus was not merely providing for His mother; He was shaping His disciple, John. Mary received a purpose. John received a blessing.

## *Reflections on Mary at the Cross Part 3*

1. When Jesus entrusted Mary to John's care, He separated her from her biological sons and daughters. How would you expect Mary to feel when told to leave her sons and possible grandchildren to stay with John?

2. How would Mary be able to help John as he and the other apostles lead the church?

**Think of Mary at the cross when:**

The challenge you are struggling with is really a blessing.

You need faith.

You leave family to serve.

# *Women at the Tomb*

*Mark 16:1-11, Matthew 28:1-10, Luke 24:1-12, John 20:1-18*

Each of the four Gospel writers includes unique details that together, create a vivid picture of this extraordinary event. While their accounts do not always follow the same sequence, the following narrative reflects my understanding of how the news of Jesus's resurrection was first announced, not by Peter, John, or the Pharisees, but by the women who had supported Him in His ministry and stood by Him through His suffering and death. The servants, the women, the last were the FIRST to hear the news! The FIRST to see and touch the risen Savior!

On the morning after the Sabbath (Sunday), before dawn, there was an earthquake, and a messenger of the Lord rolled back the stone and waited (Matthew 28:2). The women were already on their way to the tomb. I don't think they wanted to get up that morning! These women had been part of Jesus's disciples from early on. Mary Magdalene, Joanna, Mary the mother of James the less, Salome, and the other women from Galilee had listen to Jesus for over a year, had seen the miracles and were coming to Him again (Luke 24:10, Mark 16:9). Imagine the grief and the struggle to finish the task of his burial.

Without the convenience of texts or calls it is likely they had made a plan in advance. However, it's unclear if they went as a single group or if each group agreed to meet at the tomb at dawn. They may have stayed at different locations (Passover weekend) with varying distances to walk at dawn carrying the spices and ointments. John suggests Mary Magdalene arrived early (John 20:1), perhaps she was the closest. Along the way, the women wondered how they would move the stone. But the tomb was already open! The guards are missing. Inside, a young man clothed in white told them, "He is risen! He is not here. Go and tell His disciples" (Mark 16:2–8).

If Mary Magdalene arrived at the tomb first, she may have been the initial witness to its emptiness. She likely left quickly to find Peter and John, who then ran to the tomb, saw the empty grave with the burial cloths lying there, and returned to their homes (John

20:1–10). Mary, however, also returned to the tomb and remained there (John 20:11). By this time, other women had also arrived, and two men in dazzling garments appeared. Overcome with fear, the women bowed before them (Luke 24:4–5; John 20:12). The men said:

> *"Why do you seek the living among the dead? He is not here but has risen. Remember how He told you, while He was still in Galilee, that the Son of Man must be delivered into the hands of sinful men, be crucified, and on the third day rise" Luke 24:5b–7.*

Remembering Jesus's words, the women left the tomb to share the good news with the disciples. Mark mentions that some of the women were afraid and initially didn't tell anyone (Mark 16:8).

As they were leaving, a man appeared. Mary Magdelene did not recognize Him at first, but when He called her by name, she knew it was Jesus and clung to Him (John 20:11–28). Jesus also greeted the other women along the way, told them to not be afraid, to tell his brothers to go to Galilee, but He did not remain with them long (Matthew 28:8–10; Mark 16:9–11). Mary and the others returned to deliver the astonishing message, they were the very first to proclaim it to the other disciples: Jesus is risen, and we have seen Him!

Just as Elizabeth and Mary shared the news of his coming, the initial people sharing this life-changing news were not kings or religious authorities, but humble women. Those who had followed Him faithfully were the first to see the risen Savior. Yet when the other disciples heard that Jesus was alive and had appeared to them, they refused to believe it (Mark 16:9–11; Luke 24:10–12). In that moment, it must have been deeply frustrating for these women. Their testimony was dismissed. The other disciples did not believe the women who had seen Jesus.

Women at the tomb include Mary Magdalene who is mentioned by all four Gospels. Mary the mother of James, Salome, Joanna, and other women. (Matt 28:1, 5, Mark 16:1, 8, Luke 24:10, John 20:1)

## *Reflections on Women at the Tomb*

1. Jesus teaches several times that the last will be first, the first must serve - Mark 10:28-31 and Matthew 19:30 (left everything), Mark 9:33-37 and Luke 14:8-11 (humble), Matthew 20:1-28 (service). The women from Galilee, not the apostles or Pharisee or rulers, were the first to hear the good news, the first to see, and the first to touch Jesus. How does this exemplify Jesus's teachings on reversals?

2. The women from Galilee are mentioned by Luke early in Jesus's work (Luke 8:1-3). Reflect on their efforts and time with Jesus, particularly as they stood vigil at Jesus death and came to complete his burial. What were their strengths we should copy?

3. What are the weaknesses some women had who were at Jesus's tomb that we should watch in ourselves?

**Think of the Women at the tomb when:**

You are so sad you don't want to get out of bed.

You feel you are the last

People don't listen.

Jesus appears to*:*

*a. two disciples on the road to Emmaus (Luke 24:13-35, Mark 16:12-13)*
*b. Peter (Luke 24:34)*
*c. disciples without Thomas (John 20:19-23, Luke 24:36-43)*
*d. disciples with Thomas a week later (John 20:24-29)*
*e. disciples fishing at Galilee (Matthew 28:16-20)*
*f. 500 believers (1 Corinthians 15:6)*
*g. James, His brother (1 Corinthians 15:7)*
*h. apostles (Luke 24:44-49, Acts 1;3-8, 1 Corinthians 15:7)*
*i. at the Mount of Olives (Luke 24:50-53, Acts 1:9-12)*
*j. Saul (Acts 9:1-19)*

After which he delegates the teaching and service to His disciples. The Spirt is poured out and the apostles and disciples teach others about Jesus.

*"So those who received his word were baptized, and there were added that day about three thousand souls. And they devoted themselves to the apostles' teaching and the fellowship, to the breaking of bread and the prayers. And awe came upon every soul, and many wonders and signs were being done through the apostles. And all who believed were together and had all things in common." Acts 2:41-44*

Peter and John teach publicly, heal a lame man and are brought before the Jewish Council. They are released, the number of believers increase and Barnabas sells some land and gives it to the apostles to help the needy (Acts 3:2-9; 4:1,21, 36-37)

# *Sapphira*

*Acts 4:32-37, 5:1-11*

In the early days of the church, believers shared freely with one another. When needs arose some sold property to provide for those in need.

One man, Joseph, sold a piece of land and gave all the proceeds to the apostles. His generosity impressed the believers so much that they gave him a new name, Barnabas, meaning *"son of encouragement" (Acts 4:36)*. This is the same Barnabas that encouraged Saul/Paul to come and work with the church at Antioch and traveled with him establishing churches.

Ananias and Sapphira were part of the early believers and, like Barnabas, decided to sell some land and share with the church. Ananias, with Sapphira knowledge, decided to keep some of the money, but present the funds as the full price for the property. There was nothing wrong with keeping some or all of the funds; the problem was the lie. When Ananias presented the gift, he presented it as the full amount for the land, possibly hoping to gain the same admiration that Barnabas had received.

Perhaps they reasoned, *"What harm could it do? The poor still benefit, and we'll keep a little for ourselves."* But his sin was not financial, it was lying. The second mistake was assuming no one would care or know it was a lie. Peter confronted Ananias, giving him a chance to tell the truth. Instead, Ananias 'double downed' reinforcing the lie. Peter explained that money wasn't the issue, but the attempt to deceive the Holy Spirit. Ananias was seeking the appearance of highest generosity without the highest action.

Ananias may have assumed the apostles were like the temple officials or Pharisees, more interested in money than in integrity. Yet Peter made it clear that God's church is built on truth, not appearances. Just as Jesus had rebuked the Pharisees for offering money to the temple while neglecting their parents (*Mark 7:11–13*), Peter now exposed hypocrisy within the church. God demonstrated His holiness by judging Ananias, showing that a lying tongue remains something the Lord detests (*Proverbs 6:16–17*). Ananias's physical death mirrors his spiritual deadness.

A few hours later, Sapphira arrived, unaware of what had happened. She may have expected praise similar to Barnabas's. When Peter asked if the amount they gave was the full price of the land, she had an opportunity to tell the truth. But she testified falsely, supporting Ananias's deception. Like her husband, she fell under judgment, and fear came upon the whole church.

This is a tragic account of a husband and wife who, rather than strengthening one another in righteousness, conspired in deception. Had either refused to participate, the deception would have collapsed. While Scripture does not describe the dynamics of their private discussions, ultimately Sapphira chose to support the falsehood rather than reveal it.

Culture frequently sends the message that loyalty is the highest relational virtue. For example: the song, Stand by your Man; What happens in Vegas (or home), stays at Vegas; and a family first motto - puts loyalty as more important than any other actions. Covering up fraud, lying to hide abuse is 'being supportive'. Lying to authorities is 'protecting your family' and silence is 'strength'.

Some foster the idea that spouses owe each other moral immunity. Truth is negotiable if it harms the family. Some twist the teaching of marriage that 'two become one flesh' to the point that 'my guilt is your guilt', 'my enemy is your enemy', and that telling the truth becomes betrayal. Marriage does not remove individual agency, 'each of us shall give account of himself to God' (Romans 14:12). Integrity is our choice, not our spouse's.

Jesus says that following his example takes precedent over family (Luke 14:26). Telling the truth is what Sapphira should have done. It is what we should do when someone we are close to is deceiving others. Later Peter publicly declares that we must follow God rather than man (Acts 5:29). Paul warns the Ephesians not to participate in works of darkness but expose them (Eph 5:11). Loyalty is important, but not at the cost of lying or supporting fraud.

Sapphira chose to follow Christ, yet she chose loyalty to her husband over obedience to God. Her story illustrates how easy it can be to remain silent or comply rather than tell the truth.

## *Reflections on Sapphira*

1. What would happen if people were struck dead when they intentionally mislead others?

2. Can you think of an example of when truth is secondary to keeping up appearances?

3. What do you think was Sapphira's strength?

4. What was Sapphira's weakness?

**Think of Sapphira when:**

Someone expects you to lie for them.

Protecting family overrides truth

*The apostles continued to perform signs and wonders, as more people came to believe in Jesus.*

*The high priest and Sadducees move their attention to the apostles arresting and putting them in custody. An angel opens the prison and sends the apostles to the Temple to teach. The number of disciples grew. Acts 5:17-42*

# *Hellenistic widows*

*Acts 6:1*

During the feast seasons, Jews from all over the Roman world came to Jerusalem to celebrate, especially at Passover. The city was crowded, and many visitors were far from home. As the early believers shared food and resources with one another, a problem arose: the Greek-speaking Jewish widows were overlooked in the daily dispersal of food. Perhaps there was unintentional bias or simply language barriers between those who spoke Greek or Aramaic and those who spoke Hebrew.

Luke describes murmurings against the Hebrews by the Jews from outside of Judea about the Grecian widows being overlooked or disregarded. The church was using resources to take care of the needy new disciples and was struggling to be consistent.

To resolve this, the apostles appointed seven men as agents to oversee the fair distribution of supplies so that no one would be neglected. Several of these men, such as Stephen, Philip, Prochorus, Nicanor, Timon, and Parmenas, had Greek names, suggesting they were part of the Hellenistic Jewish community. This ensured the solution reflected both cultural groups and promoted unity within the church.

The plan worked well, as scripture records no further complaints. Instead, the church continued to grow, showing that wisdom, fairness, and shared responsibility strengthened the fellowship of believers.

These widows were away from home, had recognized the truth in the Gospel and became followers of Christ. Their neglect reveals the difficulty they faced as outsiders seeking inclusion. The leaders heard grumbling and delegated individuals who could communicate easily with the widows and provide help.

## *Reflections of Hellenistic women*

1. Why are people who don't speak the local language, or in the same group easy to overlook?

**Think of Hellenistic widows when:**

'Outsiders' and new people struggle to 'fit-in'.

*The church continued to grow and persecution from Jewish leaders increases. Stephen who is full of grace and power performs wonders and signs and is used as an example for punishment as he is stoned to death (Acts 6:8-15, 7).*

# *Women in prison*

*Acts 8:3, 22:4*

As the church expanded, some Jewish leaders grew alarmed. The church's growing popularity, and perhaps even the decline in offerings to the Temple, may have fueled their opposition. There were 3000 baptized after Peter's sermon (Acts 2:41). As the apostles continue to teach and help others the number rises to 5,000 (Acts 4:4). It's possible that money and influence that once flowed to traditional institutions were now being directed toward this new community of believers.

In their attempt to suppress the movement, the authorities targeted their leaders, arresting Peter and John, then Stephen, who became the first martyr (Acts 4:3, 6:8-15). After Stephen's death, Saul of Tarsus emerged as one of the most zealous persecutors of the church. Luke records that Saul went house to house, dragging off men and women and throwing them into prison (*Acts 8:3*).

This intense persecution forced many believers to scatter and become less public about their faith. These mothers, wives and sisters chose to follow Christ, and to put their lives in jeopardy. Yet even in their dispersion, the gospel continued to spread. Enforcing the message from Gamaliel who warned the Council that 'if the message is of God, you will not be able to overthrow them' (Acts 5:39).

## *Reflections on women in prison*

1. If you are thrown in prison for your belief, does it make a difference if your spouse or mother is also put in prison?

2. What are the strengths of the women and men who went to prison because they believed in Jesus?

**Think of Women in prison when:**

You don't want someone to know you are a Christian.

*For maybe one to two years, Saul fiercely persecuted followers of Jesus, targeting Jewish believers who proclaimed Him as the Messiah. Yet Jesus saw Saul's zeal and redirected it. On the road to Damascus, Saul literally "saw the light" (Acts 9:1–22; 22:6–16). Struck blind and humbled, he encountered the Lord and was transformed from persecutor to disciple.*

*Once healed and baptized, Saul began boldly preaching the gospel in Damascus and later returned to Jerusalem. His conversion shocked believers and enraged his former allies. When threats arose against his life, the Lord appeared to Saul again, instructing him to leave Jerusalem and go to the Gentiles (Acts 22:17–21). The disciples helped him escape safely to Tarsus, his hometown (Acts 9:23–30).*

*Meanwhile, after Saul's departure, the story shifts to Peter, who was ministering in Lydda. There, Peter healed a paralyzed man, leading many to faith in Christ (Acts 9:32–35). While Peter was still in Lydda, two disciples arrived from nearby Joppa, urgently asking him to come. They needed his help with a beloved believer named Tabitha.*

# *Tabitha/Dorcas*

*Acts 9:36-42*

The widows' tears tell the story of Tabitha, also known by her Greek name Dorcas. A woman from Joppa, modern-day Jaffa, which is now part of Tel Aviv. She was known for her kindness, generosity, and compassion. Tabitha didn't just feel sympathy for others; she acted on it. She cared for the poor, clothed the widows, and lived a life filled with good works and love.

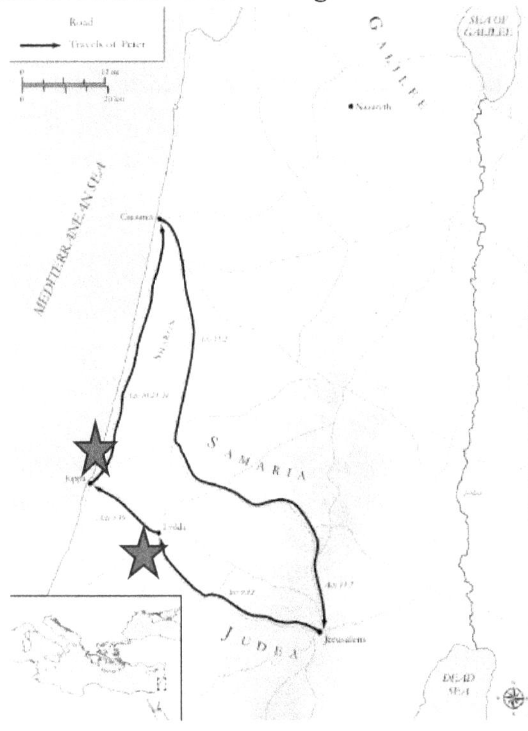


When she died, her community was heartbroken. They could not accept her loss. Unsure of what to do, they realized that Peter, an apostle of the Lord whom Tabitha had believed in, was nearby. Though they had no plan or precedent, two disciples hurried to Lydda (also called Lod), about 10–12 miles away, to ask Peter to come quickly. Since Jewish custom required burial within 24 hours, their request was urgent, born from both grief and hope.

Tabitha, their 'gazelle', had died and Tabitha's friends didn't want to lose her. When Peter arrived, he heard their weeping and saw the gifts Tabitha had shared. Peter sent everyone out of the room, then knelt and prayed beside Tabitha's body. It was a prayer of faith. Turning to her, he said simply, *"Tabitha, arise."* She opened her eyes, and when she saw Peter, he helped her to her feet.

Imagine the joy that filled the house when Tabitha was restored to life! The widows' mourning turned to rejoicing. The miracle spread throughout Joppa, and many came to believe in the Lord because of what had happened. Peter remained in the city for a time, teaching and strengthening the new believers.

Luke makes no mention of a husband or children for Tabitha; instead, the widows are the ones mourning her deeply. Their presence reminds us of James's words:

> *'Pure religion and undefiled before God... is to visit orphans and widows in their affliction,' James 1:27*

Tabitha embodied that truth. She didn't merely visit the widows, she served them, provided for them, and loved them as family. She was the kind of person communities' treasure, the mother, aunt, uncle or friend who keeps up with everyone, quietly helps where needed, and holds people together through acts of love.

## *Reflections on Tabitha*

1. What changes within the family, when the person (male or female) dies or was no longer able to be the 'glue' for the group?

2. There is some evidence that helping others is a tool to reduce stress. If true, would you expect Tabitha to be stressed? How would you describe her?

**Think of Tabitha when:**

You hear or see someone in need.

You see someone mourned by many.

You need to reduce your stress.

*From Joppa after bringing Tabitha back to her friends, Peter goes to Caesarea to talk to Cornelius, a generous Italian centurion who feared God. Peter tells Cornelius and his friends and family about Jesus and the Holy Spirit embraced the Gentiles, and they were baptized. Peter returns to Jerusalem and tells them about the Gentile Christians.*

*During a Passover Herod Agrippa (37-44 CE) seized James, the apostle, the brother of John, and had him executed. (Herod Agrippa I was a grandson of Herod the Great and nephew to Herod Antipas who had killed John the Baptist). Because killing James pleased some of the Jewish leaders, he grabbed Peter and put him in prison until after the Passover. The goal was to have him killed as he had James. However, an angel brought him out of jail and into the city. The gates open like the doors on the Starship Enterprise and Peter goes to the disciples. Acts 12:1-11*

*Herod Agrippa I was later struck down (Acts 12:20-23.)*

# *Mary, mother of John Mark and Rhoda*

Acts 12:11-17

When Peter realized he was out of jail, the first place he went was where he knew Christians would be gathered: Mary's house. This is the mother of John Mark – probably the Mark who wrote the first gospel, cousin of Barnabas, close to Peter and over time helpful to Paul (Col 4:10, 1 Peter 5:13, Acts 13:5,15:36).

Mary appears to have been related to Barnabas and was evidently well known within the early Christian community. Her home served as a gathering place for believers, and Peter instinctively went there after his release, confident it was a place of refuge. He was clearly familiar to those inside, as the servant girl Rhoda recognized his voice immediately. So overwhelmed with joy, she forgot to open the gate and ran inside to announce that Peter was standing outside, alive and free. Yet those gathered dismissed her report and refused to believe her. Peter was persistent and kept knocking until someone opened the gate. He then told them about his escape and to share the news with James (Jesus's brother) and the others. Peter then left.

Mary appears to have been a homeowner who opened her house as a gathering place for believers during a time of severe persecution from multiple sources. The Jews were persecuting the church while Herod Antipas was pursing church leaders. (Acts 12:1-4).

## *Reflections on Mary and Rhoda*

1. What strengths would Mary need to host Christians during this time?

2. Rhoda makes me smile, why would it be good to be like Rhoda?

**Think of Mary, mother of John Mark when:**

You need hospitality encouragement.

**Think of Rhoda when:**

You get so excited you forget the most important action.

People don't listen to you.

## *Roman women during the first century*

In Roman society marriage was expected of women, although there were some prominent single women and widows. Marriage among the middle and upper class typically involved a dowry. While a husband managed it during the marriage, the dowry was recognized as belonging to the wife. If the marriage ended, it was normally returned to her. In practice, many women used their dowries to cover personal expenses or to support the household. These funds gave them a measure of independence within family life (Gardner, 1991, 102).

Far from being confined to the home, Roman women appear in records as active participants in commerce. They bought and sold property, leased land, and even managed businesses. Some went further, becoming shipowners who conducted maritime trade

(Gardner, 1991, p. 233). The New Testament offers us Lydia, a merchant from Thyatira, as a vivid example. She dealt in purple cloth, one of the most valuable commodities of the time and apparently owned her own home (Acts 16:14, 40). Lydia's story highlights both her financial independence and her social influence of the time.

Roman women filled many familiar occupations. Like their Jewish counterparts, they served as shopkeepers, midwives, wet nurses, herbalists, and innkeepers. Prostitution, legal under Roman law, was another avenue by which women might earn a living, though often at great personal cost (Gardner, 1991, 133).

Although excluded from formal membership in guilds (organized groups of craftsmen and laborers) women nonetheless supported and patronized these associations (Gardner, 1991, 239). Their economic activity was visible and influential, even if the official structures of society placed limits on their direct participation.

These were the women Paul encountered in his ministry: women of means and resourcefulness, women who worked, traded, and managed their households. Paul mentions 15 women by name, only two or three that also have a husband. Some welcomed the gospel and used their resources to strengthen the Christian community, while others opposed the message. Either way, their presence was important in the spread of Christianity.

# *Devout and Prominent Women, Antioch of Pisidia*

*Acts 13:38-52*

Antioch of Pisidia was a prominent Roman colony situated in the mountains between Pisidia and Phrygia, in what is now modern-day Turkey. The city lay along a major Roman road linking the coastal regions to the interior, making it strategically important for trade and travel. As in other Roman colonies, emperor worship held a central place, and traditional Roman deities were honored and revered.

Paul and Barnabas visited Antioch of Pisidia after leaving Perga on their first mission, about 46-48 AD. In the synagogue, Paul delivered an eloquent summary of Jewish history, prophecy, and its fulfillment in Jesus Christ. Many who heard believed. The following week, nearly the entire city gathered to hear more. This stirred opposition from some Jewish leaders, who attempted to discredit Paul and Barnabas. In response, the apostles declared that since the Jewish leaders rejected the message, the good news would now be proclaimed to the Gentiles. The Gentiles rejoiced, glorifying the word of the Lord (Acts 13:13–48).

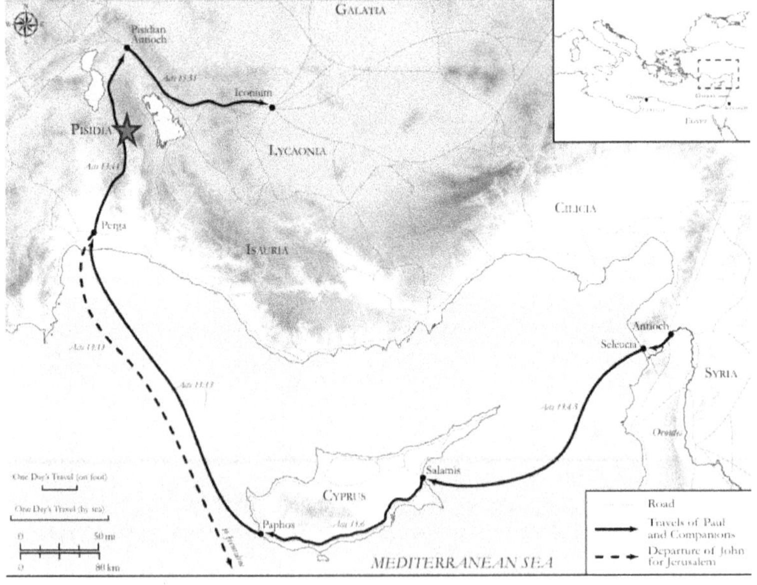

The opposition to the message of the gospel did not stop there. The Jewish leaders stirred up devout women. The word *devout* (Greek: *sebomenai*) is often used in Acts for Gentiles who worshiped the God of Israel (see *Acts 13:43; 16:14; 17:4,17*). Since the Jewish leaders had influence with them, they may have included Jehovah in their worship but were not necessarily Jewish proselytes. The need to include the women and chief men of the city to thwart Paul and Barnabas shows the power of key women in the city.

These women cared about religious issues and were influential to the extent that their power was used with the influential men of the city, to throw out Paul and Barnabas. Their combined efforts led to the persecution and eventual expulsion of the missionaries from the region. This incident indirectly highlights the significant influence women held in Roman civic and religious life, as their support was seen as crucial in driving Paul and Barnabas out of the area. Yet even in the face of hostility from both female and male leaders, the new believers in Antioch remained steadfast, filled with joy and empowered by the Holy Spirit.

## *Reflections on Devout and Prominent Women*

1. What were the strengths and possible weaknesses of these devout and prominent women?

**Think of the Devout and Prominent Women when:**

Others dictate traditions without scriptures

*Luke goes on to describe how Barnabas and Paul continued their mission through the cities of Iconium and Lystra, shadowed at times by hostile opposition from certain Jews. In Lystra, Paul was violently attacked and stoned, left for dead by the crowd. Yet, by God's strength, he rose up, recovered, and pressed forward with Barnabas to the city of Derbe. From there, the two retraced their steps, returning to Lystra, Iconium, and Antioch of Pisidia. In each place they strengthened the new believers, appointing elders, devoting themselves to prayer and fasting, and entrusting these young churches to the Lord's care. Their journey eventually brought them back to Antioch in Syria, where they reported with joy all that God had done through them (Acts 14).*

*Not long after, Paul and Barnabas traveled to Jerusalem to meet with the apostles and leaders about the expectations for Gentile believers. The church wrestled with how to welcome non-Jews and continue following Moses's Law. After the matter was resolved at the meeting in Jerusalem (Acts 15: 1-35), Paul and Barnabas planned to revisit the churches in Asia Minor. The two men split into two groups: Barnabas took John Mark and sailed for Cyprus, while Paul chose Silas and set out through Syria and Cilicia, strengthening the churches (Acts 15:36-41).*

*Paul's second mission trip was about 49 AD or almost 15 years since Jesus was resurrected. Some suggest he also wrote Galatians about this time.*

# *Lois and Eunice*

*Acts 16:1, 2 Tim 1:5, 3:15*

When Paul returned to Derbe, he met a young disciple named Timothy, the son of Eunice, a Jewish believer in Jesus, and a Greek father. Timothy already had a strong reputation among the Christians in Lystra and Iconium, and he soon joined Paul in his missionary work. It is not clear whether Eunice had embraced faith in Christ before Paul's first visit or whether she was persuaded through the ministry of Paul and Barnabas.

Years later, in Paul's final letter to Timothy, he reflects on the deep roots of Timothy's faith. He recalls the sincere devotion to God first found in Timothy's grandmother Lois, then in his mother Eunice, and now living fully in Timothy himself. Paul described this as a sincere faith (ἀνυπόκριτος, anupokritos) genuine, unpretentious, and enduring. A legacy of faith passed faithfully from one generation to the next.

Paul also reminded Timothy of his early knowledge of the Scriptures, learned from childhood in a household where God's word was studied. By the time Timothy became Paul's companion and spiritual son, he had already been shaped by the faithful lives of his grandmother and mother, women whose steady devotion prepared him for a lifetime of service.

## *Reflections on Lois and Eunice*

1. What is the value of Lois's faith?

2. What skills or traits would have helped Lois and Eunice share their faith with Timothy?

**Think of Lois and Eunice when:**

You're too tired or busy to study the Bible with children.

# *Lydia and women of Philippi*

*Acts 16:6-15;40*

In a vision, Paul is called to *"come over to Macedonia and help us"* (Acts 16:9). Obedient to this call, he and his companions travel from Troas to Neapolis and arrive at Philippi. This colonia was settled with retired Roman soldiers who had received land grants, making it a "little Rome" in both culture and loyalty. Its population included military veterans, Romans, and Greeks. The surrounding region was known for its fertile agriculture and historic gold mines.

Paul observed that Philippi lacked a synagogue, which suggested that only a small number of Jews lived in the city. Jews were distinctive in the ancient world because they observed a weekly day of rest, from Friday evening until Saturday evening, something foreign to Roman society. In the first century, the Roman calendar followed an eight-day cycle (*nundinae*), with every eighth day set aside as a market day. There was no concept of a weekend or regular day of rest. Most people, especially servants and slaves labored seven days a week.

Against this backdrop, Lydia and the women stood out. They deliberately set aside time on the Sabbath to gather at the riverside for prayer. Paul and Silas, seeking a place of worship, went outside the city gate that day and found this group. Sitting among them, they began to share the message of Jesus.

One of these women was Lydia, a dealer in purple cloth from Thyatira. Her name, Greek in origin, means "a woman from Lydia," the region around Sardis in Asia Minor. Luke describes her as a *God-fearer*, possibly a Gentile who respected the God of Israel. She may have brought members of her household with her to the gathering since they are mentioned later.

As Paul spoke, *"the Lord opened her heart to respond to his message."* This echoes other moments in Scripture when God grants spiritual sight: the disciples on the Emmaus road, for instance, whose minds Jesus *"opened to understand the Scriptures"* (Luke 24:45). Lydia likewise received divine insight to embrace the gospel. She and her household were baptized, and she immediately invited Paul and Silas to stay at her home, offering generous hospitality to strangers.

Soon after, Paul and Silas were accused of unlawful practices after casting a spirit out of a slave girl. Beaten and imprisoned, they spent the night praying and singing hymns. At midnight, an earthquake shook the prison, releasing the chains. The jailer, shaken by the event, listened to Paul's message and believed in Christ. He and his entire household were baptized that same night. Though he returned them to custody, Paul and Silas were later released. Before leaving Philippi, they returned to Lydia's house to encourage the new believers.

Lydia's hospitality and faith anchored the Philippian church. This congregation became one of Paul's strongest partners in ministry. They repeatedly supported him financially while he was in Thessalonica (Philippians 4:15), later in Corinth (2 Corinthians 11:8–9), and again during his imprisonment in Rome, when Epaphroditus delivered their gift (Philippians 2:25; 4:18).

Thus, Lydia is remembered as the first convert in Europe and a founding member of a church Paul deeply cherished. His letter to the Philippians overflows with joy, gratitude, and praise for their faith, fellowship, and steadfast partnership in the gospel.

## *Reflection on Lydia and women of Philippi*

1. What does it indicate when your household follows your lead?

2. How would you describe Lydia's strengths?

**Think of Lydia when:**

Someone asks you to meet them to pray.

Someone needs a place to stay.

You are generous.

# *Leading women of Thessalonica and Berea*

*Acts 17:1-12*

Paul and his team departed from Philippi and traveled to Thessalonica, where for three weeks he reasoned with the Jews and others. A few of the Jews were persuaded, but a great number of Greeks and many prominent women also came to believe in Jesus. Opposition soon arose from the unbelieving Jews, stirring up trouble and forcing Paul and Silas to leave for Berea.

In Berea, they again began teaching in the synagogue. The Bereans received the message eagerly, and many Jews, along with a number of respected Greek women and men, believed after verifying the teachings in the scriptures. However, the hostile Jews from Thessalonica pursued Paul even there, causing further unrest. To ensure his safety, Paul was sent to Athens, while Silas and Timothy remained behind at Berea.

## *Reflections on the Leading women of Thessalonica and Berea*

1. How would Paul and Silas talk to leading Greek women?

**Think of the women of Thessalonica and Berea when:**

You use scripture to verify teaching.

# Damaris of Athens

*Acts 17:32*

Paul, now without Silas, began teaching in Athens. After his address at the Areopagus, Luke names two individuals who embraced the gospel: Dionysius the Areopagite and a woman named Damaris. Very little is known about her, but we are told she was present, likely Greek, and that she listened to Paul and became a believer.

What is striking is that Damaris is mentioned by name apart from any husband or male relative, standing out as a single woman who responded to Paul's message. She heard of a God who created the world, does not dwell in temples made with hands, and has no need of human offerings. Paul proclaimed a God who calls all to repentance, will judge the world in righteousness, and has given assurance of this by raising Jesus from the dead (Acts 17:22–34). Damaris, Dionysius and some unnamed Greeks put their spiritual trust in the God Paul taught.

As a new believer, Damaris would have been instructed in the meaning of baptism, understood as the washing away of sins.[5]

## *Reflections on Damaris*

1. What were challenges that Damaris would have as a new Christian in Athens?

**Think of Damaris when:**

You are one of few believers.

---

[5] Ritual purification was not foreign to the Greco-Roman world. Roman religion often required cleansing before approaching the gods, whether through water, incense, or sacrifice (Plutarch, *Life of Numa* 13; Livy, *History of Rome* 1.44).

# *Priscilla*

*Acts 18: 2-4 and 18-28; Romans 16:3-5; 1 Corinthians 16:19*

Paul left Athens and traveled to Corinth, where he met Aquila and his wife Priscilla. They had recently been expelled from Rome under an edict of Claudius Caesar around AD 49. Ancient sources, including Suetonius (*Life of Claudius* 25.4), suggest the expulsion may have stemmed from disputes among Jews, possibly between those who believed in Christ and those who did not. The Jewish community later returned to Rome, likely after Claudius's death and the rise of Nero in AD 54.

Aquila and Priscilla were tentmakers by trade, the same craft Paul practiced. He stayed with them, supporting himself through tentmaking while preaching to both Jews and Gentiles about Jesus. It was likely during this time in Corinth that Paul wrote 1 and 2 Thessalonians, responding to questions they sent him.

After about eighteen months of ministry, opposition arose, and Paul departed Corinth with Priscilla and Aquila. They sailed to Ephesus, where the couple remained, while Paul continued on to Antioch, then to Galatia and Phrygia. Notably, Luke changes the order to "Priscilla and Aquila," placing Priscilla's name first in subsequent passages.

In Ephesus, Priscilla and Aquila encountered Apollos, a gifted speaker who was teaching the message of John the Baptist. They invited him to their home and explained "the rest of the story" - that John's ministry was fulfilled in Jesus Christ. Enlightened, Apollos became a bold preacher of the Gospel, encouraging the Christians in Corinth.

Paul later returned to Ephesus, teaching there for about two years and likely writing 1st Corinthians during this period. He included greetings from Priscilla, Aquila, and the church meeting in their home at Ephesus to the Christians at Corinth they had worked with previously.

Unrest eventually broke out in Ephesus, and Christians were blamed. Paul left for Macedonia and Greece, while Priscilla and Aquila seem to have returned to Rome. From Corinth, Paul wrote to the Roman church, extending warm greetings to Priscilla and

Aquila. He called them "fellow workers in Christ Jesus" who had risked their lives for him, and he added that "all the churches of the Gentiles" gave thanks for their service. He also acknowledged the church that gathered in their house at Rome.

Priscilla and Aquila emerge in Scripture as faithful and courageous leaders. They hosted churches in their homes, supported Paul's ministry at great personal risk, and taught others like Apollos. Wherever they lived in Corinth, Ephesus, or Rome, they lived as active servants of Christ, leaving a lasting mark on the early church.

## *Reflections on Priscilla*

1. What is the benefit of a strong wife and husband team in teaching the Gospel?

2. How could Priscilla and Aquilla have risked their lives for Paul?

3. What traits of Priscilla should we emulate?

**Think of Priscilla when**

People are coming and your house is dirty.

Moving requires establishing new church relationships.

# *Phoebe, Mary, Junia, Typhaena, Tryphosa, Persis, Rufus's mom, Julia, Nereus's sister*

*Romans 16:1-2, 6, 12, 13-15*

Paul likely wrote his letter to the church in Rome while staying in Corinth, during a time when Priscilla and Aquila had already returned to Rome. In his closing greetings, he mentions several women in addition to Priscilla, highlighting their important roles in the early Christian community.

Paul begins by commending Phoebe, a servant of the church at Cenchreae, Corinth's eastern port. The name Phoebe, common among wealthier Greek families, means *bright, pure, or radiant.* Paul had himself visited Cenchreae, where he had his hair cut before sailing for Syria (Acts 18:18). Many scholars believe Phoebe was entrusted with carrying Paul's letter to Rome, making her Paul's agent who delivered this epistle to the Roman believers.

Paul asks the Roman Christians to welcome Phoebe in the Lord and to assist her in whatever she might need. He describes her as a patron of many, including himself, a term suggesting she was a woman of means who provided support, relief, and encouragement to others. Some interpret Paul's use of the word "servant" (διάκονος, *diakonos*) in reference to Phoebe as evidence that she held the office of a deacon, since the same word is used in 1 Timothy 3:8–13. (see Deacon discussion in appendix.) Whether in an official role or not, she appears to have represented the Corinthian church. As an 'agent' sent by Paul she would have the qualities Paul associates with faithful service: temperance, integrity, and trustworthiness (1 Timothy 3:11). Beyond this passage, Phoebe is not mentioned again in Scripture.

In addition to Phoebe, Priscilla, and Aquila, Paul greets more than twenty-five individuals in Rome, eight of whom were women. There is a talent in noting other's efforts, and Paul frequently names those who work 'behind the scenes' and encourages them. While many may have been married, there are few couples mentioned, recognizing each individual relationship with God.

Mary is commended for her hard work on behalf of the Roman church.

Junia, greeted with Andronicus, is described as Paul's "kinsman," likely indicating Jewish heritage. Paul also notes that they were "well known among the apostles" and had been in Christ before him. This means she and Andronicus may have endured the early years of persecution, when Saul himself was imprisoning Christians (Acts 8:1), and would have known leaders like Peter and John. Paul's acknowledgment of them highlights both their faithfulness and their reconciliation with him despite his earlier hostility toward Christians.

Paul salutes several men in the group, then in verse 12, Tryphaena and Tryphosa, whose names share a root meaning *dainty* or *delicate,* are probably sisters or related. However, Paul honors them not for their delicate nature, but for their labor in the Lord.

Persis, whom Paul calls "beloved," is also recognized for her hard work in Christ. His affectionate greeting suggests a personal connection or familiarity with her in the past and knowledge of her current efforts.

Rufus is one of the men singled out as "a favorite in the Lord," and Paul warmly includes Rufus's mother, who had cared for Paul as if he were her own son.

Paul closes his greetings to those in Rome by including Philologus, Julia, Nereus and his sister, and finally Olympas and all the saints with them. Julia and Nereus's sister are mentioned, but no other information is provided. Although little detail is given about these final names, their inclusion shows the wide and diverse fellowship of believers in Rome. Jews and Gentiles together in Christ.

## *Reflection on Phoebe, Mary, Junia, Typhaena, Tryphosa, Persis, Rufus's mom, Julia, Nereus's sister*

1. What are the efforts Paul appreciates and acknowledges?

2. What did Paul ask the group to do for Phoebe?

A brief discussion on the use of Diakonos/ Diakoneo (deacon, servant, minister) is in the appendix.

**Think of Phoebe, Mary, Junia, Typhaena, Tryphosa, Persis, Rufus's mom, Julia, Nereus's sister when:**

You want to acknowledge other's efforts.

# *Philip's daughters*

*Acts 21:9*

After leaving Corinth, Paul traveled through Philippi and Troas before returning to Judea. At the coast, he stopped in Caesarea, where he stayed with Philip the evangelist, described as "one of the seven" chosen to serve in the early Jerusalem church (*Acts 6:3–5*). Philip was likely a friend of Stephen, the first Christian martyr. Remarkably, this visit took place about twenty to twenty-five years after Paul, then known as Saul, had stood approvingly at Stephen's stoning (*Acts 7:58*). Yet Philip welcomed Paul into his home with grace and hospitality.

Luke records that Philip had four unmarried daughters who prophesied (*Acts 21:9*). It's a striking detail, one Luke seems intentional in highlighting. Their ministry fulfilled the words of Joel 2:28, later quoted by Peter at Pentecost:

> *"I will pour out My Spirit on all people; your sons and your daughters will prophesy." Acts 2:17*

These young women were evidence that God's Spirit empowered both men and women to proclaim His truth. In a culture where women's voices are often limited, their prophetic role would have been both extraordinary and courageous.

Prophecy carried great responsibility. It involved speaking under the guidance of the Holy Spirit to strengthen, encourage, and comfort others (*1 Corinthians 14:3*). For Philip, raising four daughters with such a calling must have been a source of joy and a challenge, as they navigated faithfulness within a male-dominated world. Their example reminds us that God's favor is not confined by age or gender.

## *Reflection on Philip's daughters*

1. What would it have been like to be a young girl who prophesied during this time?

**Think of Philip's daughters:**

To remember that God's favor is available to all.

# *Drusilla*

*Acts 24: 22-27*

From Caesarea Paul traveled to Jerusalem, where he was attacked by a hostile mob and eventually placed in prison. When a plot against his life was uncovered, the Roman guard secretly transferred him at night to Caesarea, where he was brought before the governor, Antonius Felix.

Felix served as governor of Judea from AD 52–59 (Pilate, AD 26–36, and his successors had held the role earlier). Once a slave, Felix had been granted his freedom and rose to power. He was married to Drusilla, the daughter of Herod Agrippa I, the same king who had ordered the execution of James in Acts 12. Drusilla was also the sister of Herod Agrippa II, Berenice, and Mariamne, and a great-granddaughter of Herod the Great.

Over the course of two years, Paul spoke with Felix repeatedly. On one occasion, when Felix and Drusilla were together, Paul reasoned with them about Jesus Christ, focusing on righteousness, self-control, and the coming judgment. Felix showed interest in the message but never acted on it, becoming an example of someone intrigued by the gospel yet unwilling to change.

According to later tradition, Drusilla and her son perished in the eruption of Mount Vesuvius in AD 79.

Her sister Bernice comes to see Paul with their brother Herod Agrippa II.

## *Reflection on Drusilla*

1. What are some reasons Drusilla might have resisted becoming a Christian?

**Think of Drusilla when:**

Change is hard.

# *Bernice*

*Acts 25:13-27; Acts 26:23-32*

Bernice, daughter of Herod Agrippa I, had been married twice, both husbands having died. Afterward, she lived with her brother Herod Agrippa II, which led to rumors of an improper relationship. She later married Polemon, King of Cilicia, but soon left him and returned to live with her brother. Years later, Bernice became involved with Titus, the Roman general who destroyed Jerusalem in AD 70. Although Titus later became emperor, he refused to marry Bernice due to public disapproval in Rome.

Porcius Festus, who succeeded Felix as governor of Judea, was considered more honorable than his predecessor, though he served only two or three years. During this time, around AD 60–62, Paul was brought before Festus, Herod Agrippa II, and Bernice to make his defense. Paul boldly shared his testimony and the message of the gospel.

Agrippa admitted that Paul's appeal was persuasive, saying,

> *'With but little persuasion thou wouldest fain make me a Christian'. Acts 26:28*

Yet he refused to act. After conferring together, Festus, Agrippa, and Bernice agreed that Paul had done nothing deserving death or imprisonment. However, because he had appealed to Caesar, Paul was sent to Rome.

Luke includes Bernice among those who listened to Paul's defense, but Scripture records no response of faith. Her silence, and later choices, suggest that, though she heard the truth, she never pursued it.

## *Reflection on Bernice*

1. When you are called to act, but you choose not to act; what does that indicate?

**Think of Bernice when:**

You choose not to change.

# *Euodias and Syntyche*

*Philippians 4:2-3*

Paul eventually made his way to Rome, where he wrote several letters during his imprisonment (around AD 62 and after). Among the churches he corresponded was the Philippian church, located in the region of Macedonia. Paul often praised them for their remarkable generosity in helping others, as noted in 2 Corinthians 8:1–5 and Romans 15:26. His letter to them shines with joy and reflects his deep confidence in their maturity and faithfulness in Christ.

In his closing words, Paul turns to a concern involving two women in the congregation, urging them "to be of the same mind in the Lord." While Euodias ("good path") and Syntyche ("good fortune") may have differed on many issues, Paul reminds them that their unity in Christ must be their foundation. The disagreement was significant enough that Epaphroditus, who brought news from Philippi (Philippians 2:25-30), apparently made Paul aware of it. Yet Paul does not take sides, nor does he direct the church to enforce a solution. The conflict appears not to be about doctrine, but something more personal. Instead, Paul appeals to the whole church, his 'true yokefellows', to come alongside these women, offering help and support rather than standing by in silence.

Importantly, Paul honors both Euodias and Syntyche as fellow laborers in the gospel, alongside Clement and many others. They had contended at Paul's side, indicating active roles and not peripheral members. He reassures them that their names are written in the book of life, a reminder that even in conflict, they remain beloved, secure in Christ, and part of God's eternal family.

Conflicts among believers still happen today. This was not a rebuke for false teaching, but an example of helping others work through personal differences. They had worked together in the past and Paul calls them to focus on what they share in Christ, so that God would be glorified through their unity.

## *Reflections on Euodias and Syntyche*

1. How does keeping our eyes on the bigger picture of the gospel help us handle personal disagreements?

**Think of Euodias and Syntyche when:**

Your disagreements keep you from glorifying God.

# Apphia

*Philemon 1:1-2*

Philemon is a brief, personal letter addressed to Philemon, Apphia (likely his wife), Archippus, and the church that meets in their home, probably delivered alongside Paul's letter to the wider congregation at Colossae (the letter to the Colossians). In it, Paul explains that Onesimus, Philemon's enslaved servant, has become a Christian and is returning to Philemon's house as more than a servant, a beloved brother. Paul acknowledges any wrong or debt Onesimus may owe and offers to cover it himself, expressing confidence that Philemon will respond generously.

Apphia is named in the greeting, suggesting her active role in the household. If she is the wife, she probably was important to providing the church's hospitality at Colossae. Like Martha, Priscilla, Nympha, Lydia, and Mary (the mother of John Mark), Apphia hosted and supported early Christian gatherings in her home.

## *Reflections on Apphia*

1. How do you feel about having a church meet at your house every week?

**Think of Apphia when:**

You need encouragement in hospitality

*After Paul's first imprisonment in Rome, many scholars believe he was released and resumed visiting several of the churches he had founded, writing 1 Timothy and Titus, possibly from Ephesus. Meanwhile, the Roman Empire entered a turbulent period. Between AD 66 and 79, five emperors: Nero, Galba, Otho, Vitellius, and Vespasian rose and fell in quick succession, creating widespread instability.*

*In AD 66, a Jewish revolt erupted when Zealots seized control of Jerusalem and expelled the Roman garrison. That same year, Emperor Nero blamed the great fire of Rome on Christians, unleashing a brutal wave of persecution. After this Paul was possibly arrested again, and during this final imprisonment, around AD 67–68, he possibly wrote 2 Timothy.*

*During these years, General Vespasian and his son Titus led Roman campaigns through Judea, subduing Galilee by AD 68. In AD 70, during the Passover season, Titus surrounded Jerusalem. The siege brought famine, despair, and immense suffering before Roman troops finally breached the walls and burned the Temple. This event marked a decisive turning point in Jewish history: the priestly and sacrificial system ended, and worship shifted permanently to the synagogues and the study of Torah under rabbinic leadership.*

*By this time, some of the New Testament writings were already circulating among the churches. Luke had probably composed his Gospel and Acts for Theophilus. Both Peter and Paul were likely executed during Nero's persecution, so their writings were complete. With Jerusalem in ruins, Titus became emperor, and the Jewish people were scattered throughout the empire.*

# *Favorite Lady*

*2 John 1*

John, now advanced in age, was possibly living in Ephesus and continued writing to strengthen and guide the churches. In *2 John*, he addressed "the favorite lady and her children," a phrase that some interpret as a symbolic reference to a local congregation, while others see it as a personal letter to a woman who hosted a church at her home. The letter likely dates from the mid to late 80s AD, during the reign of Emperor Domitian.

Domitian insisted that subjects address him as "Lord and God," which put Christians in direct conflict with imperial expectations. Those who refused were persecuted, so John may have used indirect or affectionate language, such as "the favorite lady and her children", to protect readers from scrutiny.

John commends believers who "walk in truth," reminding them that genuine love must always be expressed within the boundaries of truth. He rejoices that her "children" walk faithfully, whether literal family members or spiritual disciples she had nurtured in faith. Yet John also warns against welcoming false teachers who deny that Jesus came in the flesh, a growing issue in the early church. His message blends tenderness with discernment: love others deeply, but never at the expense of truth.

He concludes the letter by expressing his desire to speak face-to-face rather than through writing, and he sends greetings from "the children of your chosen sister", perhaps another congregation or a close spiritual companion.

## *Reflections on Favorite Lady*

1. What would be the strengths of the Favorite Lady?

2. What are areas the Favorite Lady should watch?

**Think of the Favorite Lady when:**

You are tired and don't want to train your child.

Truth and discernment are needed.

# Jezebel

*Revelations 2:18-23*

Jesus shared his thoughts on the seven churches to John, the remaining apostle. This would have been about 85-96 AD close to the time of John's other letters.

The churches addressed in Revelation possibly shared a postal route from Ephesus in the western area of Turkey. Thyatira was located between Pergamum and Sardis, which is reflected in their order in John's letter (Ephesus, Smyrna, Pergamum, Thyatira, Sardis, Philadelphia, and Laodicea).

Jesus was sharing with John and the churches feedback on what they were doing well and where they needed to improve. We previously learned about Lydia who lived in Phillipi and had come from Thyatira as a seller of purple (Acts 16:12,14). Textile dyeing was one of the products from Thyatira.

Jesus saw the love, faith, service and patient endurance of the church at Thyatira; and how it had grown. An outstanding recommendation, and pat on the back. But the issue with the church at Thyatira is that they tolerated Jezebel.

Women's names in the city of Thyatira were usually from Greek or Roman names. Most scholars suggest that Jezebel in this case was a pseudonym used by John to suggest the character and influence of this person.

In the Old Testament, Jezebel was a daughter of the King of Sidon from the area of Phoenicia who married King Ahab (1 Kings 16:31). Through her influence the prophets of Jehovah were killed or banned from Isreal while prophets of Baal ate at her table (1 Kings 18:4,13, 19). She had Naboth killed so Ahab could have his vineyard (1 Kings 21:7, 15). She generally stirred up Ahab to evil (1Kings 21:25). Jezebel promoted the worship of foreign gods, corruption and violence to achieve her goals, and suppressed or killed Jehovah's prophets. She became a symbol of idolatry, false teaching and religious fusion, reshaping Israel's worship to fit with other kingdoms.

The woman in Revelations followed Jezebel's pattern of false teachings, idolatrous influence, and sexual immorality. She was blending Christianity with idolatry and fornication (syncretism). Jezebel maintained the practices of the culture and joined with the 'new' group call Christians. She called herself a prophet. She was showing how followers could maintain their practice of idolatry and follow the teachings of Christ.

Jesus calls out the lie that she is a prophet. A true prophet's words align with God's revealed truth and come to pass (Deuteronomy 18:22). The woman called "Jezebel" does not align her teachings with truth. Instead, she promotes teachings that directly oppose the moral and doctrinal standards of Christ (*Revelation 2:20*).

The second issue Jesus condemns is her teaching and seducing believers to engage in sexual immorality and to eat food sacrificed to idols (*Rev. 2:20*). Thyatira was a city tied to trade guilds, and each guild had its own patron deity. Participation in guild feasts, where meat offered to idols was served, was expected for economic and social success.

Paul had earlier written that eating such food was not sinful in itself (*1 Corinthians 8:4–9*), but joining in pagan rituals was incompatible with Christian faith (*1 Corinthians 10:20–21*). Jezebel appears to have blurred that line, encouraging believers to mix Christian identity with old pagan customs, possibly justifying compromise as harmless.

Her teaching allowed participation in sexual practices common in idol worship, acts that were part of the fertility rites of deities like Apollo or Artemis, both venerated in Thyatira. She seems to have promoted inclusion and personal freedom over obedience and holiness.

Jesus makes it clear that she knew what repentance required and had been given time (Revelation 2:21). She claimed to be part of the church while encouraging others to join her in actions contrary to Jesus's teachings. Like many today, she wanted to belong to the Christian community but on her own terms, seeking admiration and followers rather than service.

What is striking is that the church had allowed her influence to spread. Instead of confronting her actions, they tolerated her leadership. Jesus holds both Jezebel and those participating accountable:

> *'Behold, I cast her into a bed, and them that commit adultery with her into great tribulation, except they repent of her works.' Rev. 2:22*

The church at Thyatira is warned that tolerance of false teaching is not love. A group that excuses sin or accommodates those who lead others astray becomes complicit in the harm. Jezebel joined the church but sought power and influence not repentance and change.

## *Reflections on Jezebel*

1. Why would a group filled with love, faith, service, and patience in Thyatira tolerate Jezebel and her followers?

2. What were the traits that the woman called 'Jezebel' shows?

**Think of Jezebel when:**

You want to be with Christians without giving up your sin.

You hear sin and serving Christ is compatible.

# Remember…

**When people don't listen**, remember Rhoda was dismissed when she said Peter stood at the door. Pilate ignored his wife's warning that Jesus was righteous. Even after the empty tomb, the disciples did not believe the women who said Jesus had risen.

**When life does not unfold as expected**, remember Elizabeth's long barrenness before God gave her John. Remember Mary, who likely never imagined fleeing to Egypt, hiding from Herod, or watching her Son rejected.

**When it feels that prayers are unheard**, remember Anna's years of worship and waiting. Remember Elizabeth and Zechariah receiving a son in old age. Remember the woman suffering twelve years with bleeding who came to Jesus, and the Canaanite mother who persisted for her daughter.

**When pride or grudges take root**, remember Herodias and the destruction they caused. And remember the Canaanite woman, who set aside pride and received mercy.

**When you feel worthless**, remember the weeping sinner, the Samaritan woman, and the woman caught in adultery, people who learned that God sees and cares.

**When you feel too busy to teach the next generation**, remember Lois and Eunice who taught Timothy, and the beloved lady John commended for walking in truth with her children.

**When you are tempted to go along with wrongdoing**, remember Sapphira who chose deception. And if you wish to claim Christ while clinging to sin, remember the warning against the woman called Jezebel in Thyatira.

**When grief feels overwhelming**, remember the widow of Nain, Mary and Martha at Lazarus' tomb, and the women who stood near the cross.

**When suffering makes worship difficult**, remember the woman bent over for eighteen years who still came to the synagogue, and the woman who pressed through the crowd to touch Jesus.

**When fear tempts you to stay silent about Jesus**, remember the blind man's parents who would not speak, and the women who were imprisoned because they did.

**When you focus on resources for the future**, remember the widow who gave all she had at the temple, trusting God for her daily bread.

**Remember we are not alone.**

# Appendix

Historical background is included to give context, but not as a historical source. So historical details should be read with care and not assumed to apply to all people or regions. The dates are estimates, and most of the information in this section is from Encyclopedia Britannica and Wikipedia.

## *Rulers from 400 BCE to 100 CE*

### Government up to Jesus's birth

After Cyrus of Persia permitted the Jews to return from Babylon (Ezra 1:1–2), they rebuilt the Temple and the walls of Jerusalem under Nehemiah's leadership. Ezra reestablished the Law and restored the priesthood, though the region remained under Persian rule from approximately 540 to 430 BCE.

In the following century, Macedonian and Greek influence spread throughout the region, culminating in Alexander the Great's conquest of Persia by 332 BCE. After his death, his empire was divided among his generals, continuing Greek (Hellenistic) rule.

By 164 BCE, the Maccabees led a successful revolt in Judea, establishing Hasmonean rule, which lasted until 63 BCE, when Pompey of Rome intervened in a civil conflict among Jewish leaders and brought the region under Roman control. The Maccabees continued to be the named ruler, but they reported to Rome until they were replaced by Herod the Great in 37 BCE.

Pompey was a member of the First Roman Triumvirate, along with Julius Caesar and Crassus. By 49 BCE, Julius Caesar had seized control of the Roman Republic, but his rule was cut short when he was assassinated on the Ides of March (March 15, 44 BCE) by Brutus, Cassius, and other senators.

In response, Octavian (Caesar's adopted heir) joined forces with Mark Antony and Lepidus to form the Second Triumvirate, aiming to avenge Caesar's death. Their alliance succeeded militarily, and during this period, Mark Antony supported Herod, who, backed by

Rome, overthrew the last Hasmonean ruler and was declared "King of the Jews" under Roman authority (37 BCE).

Over time, Lepidus faded from power, and tensions grew

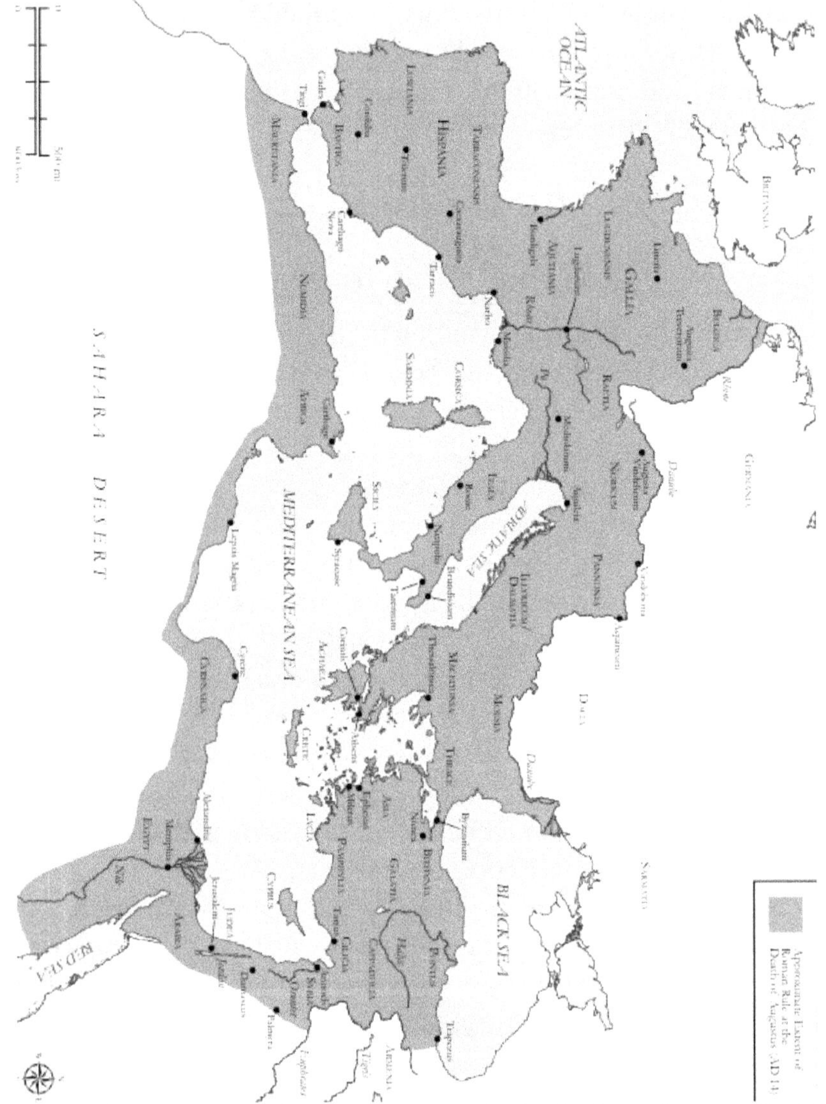

between Octavian and Mark Antony, who had aligned himself with Cleopatra of Egypt. The rivalry culminated in the Battle of Actium in 31 BCE, where Octavian decisively defeated Antony and Cleopatra. Both took their own lives shortly thereafter.

In 27 BCE, Octavian was granted the title Augustus Caesar and became the emperor of Rome. He ruled until his death in 14 CE, when Jesus would have been a young boy or teenager. Power then passed peacefully to Tiberius.

| Roman Ruler | Reign | Notes |
|---|---|---|
| **Julius Caesar** | 49–44 BCE | Assassinated; granted citizenship to some Jews |
| **Octavian (Augustus Caesar)** | 27 BCE – 14 CE | First official emperor |
| **Tiberius** | **14–37 CE** | Emperor during Jesus's ministry (Luke 3:1). |
| **Caligula (Gaius Caesar)** | 37–41 CE | Demanded worship as a god |
| **Claudius** | 41–54 CE | Expelled Jews from Rome (Acts 18:2) |
| **Nero** | 54–68 CE | Persecuted Christians |
| **Galba** | June 68 – Jan 69 CE | First in the "Year of Four Emperors." |
| **Otho** | Jan – Apr 69 CE | Brief reign during civil war. |
| **Vitellius** | Apr – Dec 69 CE | Very brief; unstable period. |
| **Vespasian** | 69–79 CE | Led Roman army during Jewish Revolt |
| **Titus** | 79–81 CE | Destroyed the Second Temple (70 CE) |
| **Domitian** | 81–96 CE | Enforced emperor worship. |
| **Nerva** | 96–98 CE | More moderate; brief reign. |
| **Trajan** | 98–117 CE | Began expansionist policies |

Tiberius was financially conservative and avoided unnecessary wars, focusing on order and stability. However, he was distrustful and had many political enemies. He retreated from a public role in

26 CE and left the government and 'autopen' to others. While Tiberius is listed as the ruler during Jesus's trial and death, he wasn't considered very active during this period. Tiberius died in 37 CE and was succeeded by Caligula.

Luke 3:1 mentions that John the Baptist began his public ministry during the 15th year of Tiberius's reign, around 29 CE. The rulers were an unengaged Tiberius over the Roman Empire, Pontius Pilate governed Judea, Samaria, and Idumea (he began in 26 CE), Herod Antipas controlled Galilee and Perea, and Herod Philip II ruled the northeastern territories.

| Judean Territory | | |
|---|---|---|
| **Pompey took Roman Control** | | 63 BCE |
| **Multiple Hasmonean rulers under Roman control** | | 63-37 BCE |
| **Herod the Great** | King of Judea (Rome-appointed) | 37 BCE to 4 CE |
| **Herod Archelaus** | Ethnarch of Judea – replaced by Prefects | 4 BCE – 6 CE |
| **Herod Antipas** | Tetrarch of Galilee & Perea | 4 BCE – 39 CE |
| **Herod Philip II** | Tetrarch of Iturea | 4 BCE – 34 CE |
| **Herod Agrippa I** | King over all Judea (Acts 12:1,20) | 37–44 CE |
| **Herod Agrippa II** | Tetrarch & king over parts | 50s–c. 100 CE |

The Prefects replaced Herod Archelaus over Judea. Pontius Pilate, Antonius Felix and Porcius Festus are mentioned by the New Testament writers which helps estimate dates of some events.

## Roman Prefects over Judah

| PREFECT/PROCURATOR | **REIGN** |
|---|---|
| Coponius | 6–9 CE |
| Marcus Ambivulus | 9–12 CE |
| Annius Rufus | 12–15 CE |
| Valerius Gratus | 15–26 CE |
| **Pontius Pilate** | 26–36 CE |
| Marcellus | 36–37 CE |
| Marullus | 37–41 CE |
| Cuspius Fadus | 44–46 CE |
| Tiberius Alexander | 46–48 CE |
| Ventidius Cumanus | 48–52 CE |
| **Antonius Felix** | 52–59 CE |
| **Porcius Festus** | 59–62 CE |
| Lucceius Albinus | 62–64 CE |
| Gessius Florus | 64–66 CE (His cruelty helped spark the First Jewish Revolt) |

In 66–73 CE, a Jewish Revolt broke out, ending in the destruction of the Temple in 70 CE by Roman General (later Emperor) Titus. (dates are estimates) See Josephus, Antiquities 18-20 and War 2.

# Government after Herod the Great's death

Ceaser Augustus continued to rule Rome and divided Herod the Great's territory at his death among his sons:

A. Herod Archelaus ruled Judea, Samaria, and Idumea from 4 BCE to 6 CE. Within a couple of years his cruelty and abuse were so bad Rome removed him, replacing him with Roman prefects. Pontius Pilate became the Prefect most known since he served from around 26 to 36 CE during Jesus's ministry. A list of prefects during this time is listed previously.

B. Herod Antipas ruled Galilee and Perea from 4 BCE to 39 CE. He married a Nabataean princess as a political alliance. He visited Rome and stayed with his half-brother Herod Philip I and Herodias. He persuaded Herodias to leave Herod Philip I and marry him. However, he also had to divorce his Nabatean wife, which created political problems for him later (Josephus, *Antiquities* 18.5.1–2).

   Herodias was the granddaughter of Herod the Great. Her first husband was Herod Philip I (Not the Philip who ruled Batanea). This is the Herodias who had John the Baptist executed.

   Herod Antipas eventually ordered the execution of John the Baptist (Mark 6). He was also in Jerusalem during the Passover and met Jesus during His trial (Luke 23).

C. Herod Philip II (Philip the Tetrarch) was another half-brother to Herod Antipas and ruled Batanea and surrounding regions in modern Syria from 4 BCE to 34 CE. He was considered a fair and good ruler. Later in life he married Salome (his niece and former dancer), the daughter of Herodias and Herod Philip I. They did not have any children.

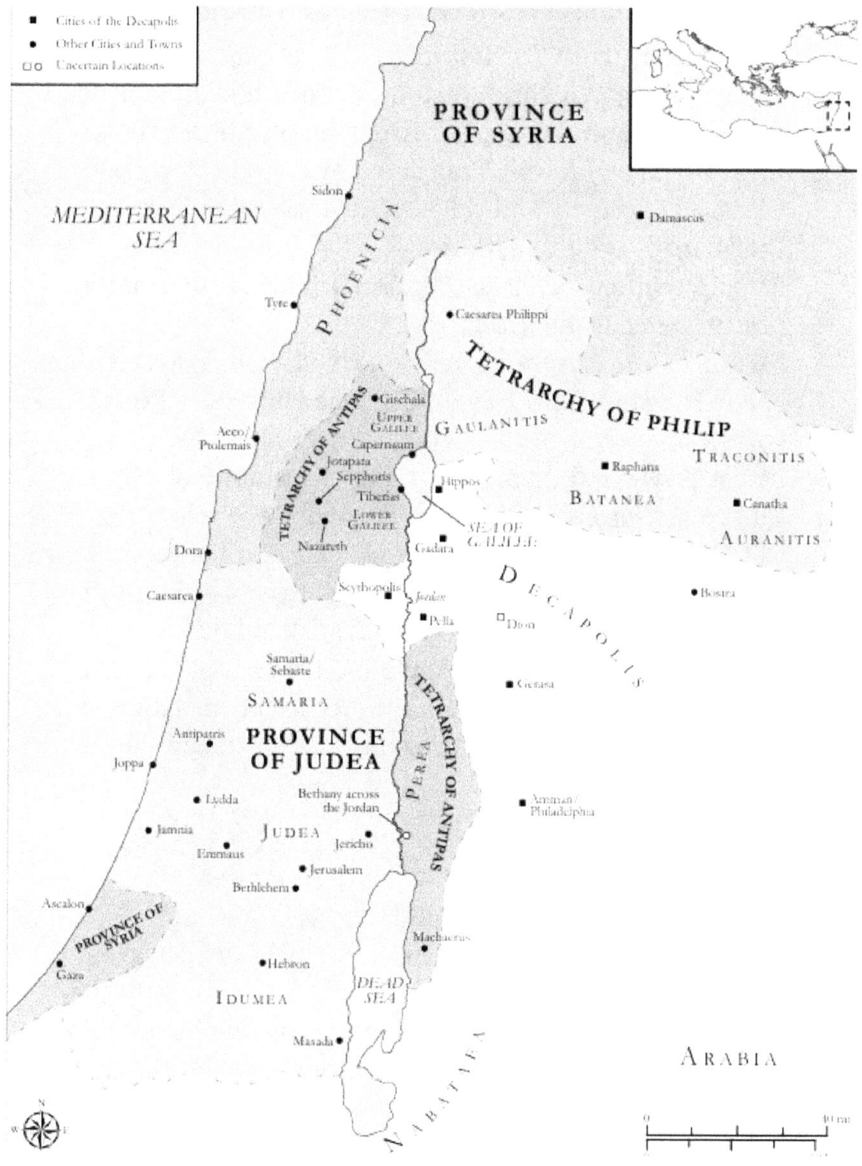
Cities of the Decapolis
Other Cities and Towns
Uncertain Locations
PROVINCE OF SYRIA
MEDITERRANEAN SEA
Sidon
Damascus
PHOENICIA
Tyre
Caesarea Philippi
TETRARCHY OF PHILIP
TETRARCHY OF ANTIPAS
Gischala
UPPER GALILEE
GAULANITIS
Acco/ Ptolemais
Capernaum
Jotapata
Sepphoris
Tiberias
Hippos
Raphana
TRACONITIS
BATANEA
Canatha
LOWER GALILEE
SEA OF GALILEE
Nazareth
Gadara
AURANITIS
Dora
DECAPOLIS
Caesarea
Scythopolis
Jordan
Bostra
Pella
Dion
Samaria/ Sebaste
SAMARIA
Gerasa
TETRARCHY OF ANTIPAS
Antipatris
PROVINCE OF JUDEA
Joppa
PEREA
Lydda
Bethany across the Jordan
Amman/ Philadelphia
Jamnia
JUDEA
Jericho
Emmaus
Jerusalem
Bethlehem
Ascalon
PROVINCE OF SYRIA
Machaerus
Gaza
Hebron
DEAD SEA
IDUMEA
Masada
ARABIA
NABATAEA

# *Bibliography*


**Primary Ancient Sources (Modern Translations)**

1. Josephus, Flavius. *The Complete Works of Josephus*. Translated by William Whiston, revised and edited by Paul L. Maier. Grand Rapids, MI: Kregel Publications, 1999.
2. Livy. *History of Rome*. Translated by B. O. Foster. Loeb Classical Library. Cambridge, MA: Harvard University Press, 1919–1959 1.44, 8, 10. https://scaife.perseus.org/reader/urn:cts:latinLit:phi0914.phi001.perseus-eng3:1.44
3. Mishnah. *The Mishnah: A New Translation*. Translated by Jacob Neusner. New Haven, CT: Yale University Press, 1988. https://www.sefaria.org/Mishnah_Yevamot.6.6?lang=bi
4. Plutarch. *Lives*. Translated by Bernadotte Perrin. Loeb Classical Library. Cambridge, MA: Harvard University Press, 1914–1926. https://topostext.org/work/651?utm
5. Suetonius. *The Twelve Caesars*. Translated by Robert Graves. Rev. ed. London: Penguin Classics, 2007. (See *Life of Claudius*, 25.4.) Also from the J.C. Rolf translation and Lexundria. https://lexundria.com/suet_cl/25.4/r?utm

**Secondary Sources**

6. Franklin, Benjamin. *Poor Richard's Almanack*. Philadelphia: Benjamin Franklin, 1736. https://en.wikisource.org/wiki/Poor_Richard%27s_Almanack?utm
7. Gardner, Jane F. *Women in Roman Law and Society*. Bloomington: Indiana University Press, 1991.
8. Ilan, Tal. *Jewish Women in Greco-Roman Palestine*. Peabody, MA: Hendrickson Publishers, 1996.
9. McCormack, Laura K. C. "Education for Girls in Ancient Rome." *World History Encyclopedia*, February 6, 2025. https://www.worldhistory.org

# *Deacon word study*

Some suggest that Phoebe held the title and office of a Deacon in Romans 16:1.

*I commend unto you Phoebe our sister, who is a* *<u>servant</u>* *of the church that is at Cenchrea:*

The New International Version, Ya'll Bible Version, New Living Translation and New Revised Standard Versions use the title deacon to describe Phoebe in this passage.

My current understanding of the title deacon as described in the New Testament scriptures is summarized below:

1. Scriptures describing roles in the New Testament don't mention deacons: Ephesians 4:11-15, 1 Corinthians 12:27-31, Acts 14:23, Acts 20:28, 1 Peter 5:1-3 and Titus 1:5-9. The fact that the title or office of a Deacon is not listed with other roles in the New Testament seems to indicate it was not a recognized title when the books were written.

2. The men selected in Acts 6:1, 4 are not given any title or called Deacons at the time of their service or years later. Philip, 'one of the seven' is called an evangelist, not a deacon (Acts 21:8). They are given specific work and have specific character requirements. There is no title given to the men in Acts in the scriptures.

3. The King James linguists who translated the Bible into English <u>transliterated</u> a few words. (Created an English word from the Greek rather than translate the meaning, for example: Baptize, Angel, Deacon, etc.). Diakonos/ Diakoneo is <u>transliterated</u> to deacon in 2 passages. Philippians 1:1 and 1 Timothy 3:8, 10, 12, 13.) The other 53 times the words are used in the New Testament, they are translated as servant or minister.
    a. I suspect that there were men with the title of 'Deacon' in roles of the Anglican Church (Church of England) at this time. Therefore, the translators created the title in 1

Timothy 3:8-13 and Philippians 1:1 to support current practice.

4. Paul frequently used the term servant or minister (deacon, Diakonos/ Diakoneo) referring to himself (1 Corinthians 3:5; 2 Corinthians 3:6; 6:4; 11:23; Ephesians 3:7; Colossians 1:23, 25), Apollos (1 Corinthians 3:5), Timothy (1 Timothy 4:6), Epaphras (Colossians 1:7), Tychicus (Ephesians 6:21; Colossians 4:7), and Phoebe (Romans 16:1). This indicates a term of work, not title or leadership.

5. In Paul's discussion, the Greek word gunē in 1 Timothy 3:11 can be translated women or wives depending on the context. ASV uses women, most other translations use wives. In studying the women of the New Testament, it is revealing how many women are mentioned alone in their discipleship. Phoebe went from Corinth to Rome apparently without a husband. Therefore, it does not seem unusual for Paul to include women in this discussion, not wives. (Note: Paul's description of Phoebe in Romans was probably written before his letter to Timothy.)

6. It seems inconsistent to expect the wives of deacons (servants) to have requirements when elder/overseer qualifications in 1 Timothy 3:1-7 or in Titus 1:5-9 passages do not have any expectations for their wives. Why would Paul expect deacon wives to be grave, not slanderers, temperate, and faithful but have no expectations for the wife of the overseer/elder?

Using the Greek definition rather than transliteration title indicates that Paul was not adding a new office or leadership position in 1 Timothy 3:8-13. He was making sure Timothy didn't have anyone representing the church without a 'background check'. Paul understood the concept of 'agency' and how representatives reflect on the group. Having those representing the church be reviewed for key qualities is something most realize is important.

Below are the 'Deacon' passages translating the words Diakonos/ Diakoneo to servant or minister.

*Paul and Timothy, servants of Christ Jesus, to all the saints in Christ Jesus that are at Philippi, with the bishops and servants: (Philippians 1:1)*

*Servants in like manner must be grave, not double-tongued, not given to much wine, not greedy of filthy lucre; holding the mystery of the faith in a pure conscience. And let these also first be proved; then let them serve, if they be blameless.*

*Women in like manner must be grave, not slanderers, temperate, faithful in all things.*

*Let servants be husbands of one wife, ruling their children and their own houses well.*

*For they that have served well gain to themselves a good standing, and great boldness in the faith which is in Christ Jesus.*

*1 Timothy 3:8-13*

Paul is telling Timothy that whoever represents the church should meet certain criteria. Think of a real estate agent. If they represent you, they should have integrity, be honorable, etc. An agent who lies will associate you with their lies.

The church also needs to make sure those being entrusted with funds, letters, etc. meet a minimum guideline. It is not a leadership role, but a servant role for men and women. No title, no office, no leadership training position. Phoebe was representing the church at Cenchrea (the port at Corinth). Paul is vouching for her to the Christians at Rome. He later tells Timothy that servants representing the church should meet some qualifications.

For those who question the requirement for servant representatives and elders to have one wife, remember Jewish law allowed polygamy. While there are periods when it was not practiced frequently, it was still in Moses's law. Paul is reminding the Jewish Christians that polygamy is not an option for Christians.

# Questions and suggested responses

These are some possible answers to the questions. You will probably have better responses, but I hope these help us think about the challenges, strengths and weaknesses of the women discussed in the New Testament. These are my opinions.

### Reflection on Elizabeth

1. As a daughter of the sons of Aaron, Elizabeth would have been a highly regarded bride. But she describes herself as having *'reproach'* for her childlessness. Have you ever felt dejected in how others see you because of unmet expectations or delayed hopes? How could Elizabeth's story help you?

*Elizabeth persevered. She felt the reproach but pushed forward as a wife and follower of God. Though faithfulness isn't always rewarded quickly, God had not forgotten her. Elizabeth became the mother of John, who Jesus refers to as great, not a term used frequently (Matthew 11:11, Luke 7:28). Elizabeth's story reminds us that even in silence and waiting, God's plans are still unfolding for those who continue to follow him.*

2. Elizabeth went from feeling disgraced to having a miraculous pregnancy. Her son would be a prophet like Elijah! You can feel her joy.... Then, a teen girl comes who has an even more miraculous pregnancy. What was Elizabeth's response to Mary's news that her son would be the Messiah? What were some reactions we might have when other's news overshadows us?

*It is easy to feel minimized, competitive or resentful, but Elizabeth recognized God as the source. She did not show envy at Mary's news, but responded with joy, humility and blessing. Mary was welcomed into her home. She believed Mary's story when Mary probably needed support and kindness the most.*

3. Based on her actions and those around her, what are Elizabeth's strengths?

*a) Elizabeth is righteous and faithful, obeying God's commandments even as she lives with the disappointment of childlessness.*
*b) She apparently had a strong marriage since Zechariah did not take another wife.*
*c) Her perseverance is evident in her continued devotion amid disappointment*
*d) Her humility shines when she recognizes Mary as the mother of her Lord and her lesser role. (Just as John did with Jesus.)*
*e) Elizabeth would have encouraged a young, possibly scared Mary.*
*f) Elizabeth is filled with the Holy Spirit and speaks prophetic words of blessing and affirmation. This probably offers emotional and spiritual support to a vulnerable Mary, creating trust and providing encouragement.*
*g) John became great (Matthew 11:11, Luke 7:28), but Elizabeth would be a part of his life and share her faith. She was a nurturer!*

*Furthermore, her obedience is clear when she insists on the name John, following the direction given by God despite others trying to ignore her and cultural expectations to name the son after the father.*

## Reflection on Mary: You will have a son

1. Mary asks how she will conceive since she is a virgin. What does that question tell you about Mary?

*Mary seemed to have accepted the idea and had moved on to how. She seems calm and practical. Think of a teenage girl you know, how do you think she would respond?*
*Zechariah struggled to believe Gabriel, but Mary seems to accept it. I think teen girls are possibly easier to convince they have been chosen for something special than older people. Youth has an optimism that may decline as we age.*

2. There is an old saying: Man plans, and God laughs. How do you feel when you have everything planned out and God changes it?

*I'm a planner, so initially it is annoying and frustrating to have things not go as I want them. So, thinking about Mary and*

*Jephthah's daughter helps me keep myself in perspective – sometimes.*

3. From these few verses what are some of Mary's strengths?

- *Mary recognized the power of Gabriel, and what he was asking quickly (Discernment)*
- *She stayed calm and practical.*
- *She refers to herself as the Lord's bondservant which indicates her humility.*
- *Her prayer shows her grasp of God.*

## Reflections on Mary visits Elizabeth

1. Why did Mary hurry to visit Elizabeth after Gabriel's message?

*Mary may have wanted to confirm Gabriel's message and to help her older relative Elizabeth. Despite her faith, she likely desired to witness the miracle Gabriel spoke of firsthand.*

2. Visiting someone uninvited for 3 months: What kind of friendship did Mary and Elizabeth share?

*I wonder if Elizabeth was friends with Mary's mother, and their friendship grew over this time. Their bond was intergenerational, between a young woman and an older woman, rooted in shared faith, miraculous pregnancies, and deep spiritual understanding.*
*I hope that Elizabeth and Mary were able to see each other later, at feasts and maybe when Mary lived in Bethlehem. There is no scripture, just a thought.*

3. What insight does Mary's response (Magnificat) to Elizabeth give us about her heart and faith?

*Mary's response (Luke 1:46–55) reveals her deep joy, humility, and understanding of God's character. Her words show gratitude, reverence, and an awareness of God's justice and mercy. She seems to have a greater understanding of God's attitude and purpose than many of us.*
*Joy and praise to God*
*Humble acceptance of God's favor*

*God's mercy to those who fear Him*
*God's reversal of worldly status: humbling the proud, exalting the lowly*
*God's faithfulness to Abraham's descendants*

4, What are some strengths Mary exhibited in these passages? Did you see any weaknesses?

- *Mary did not wait to go see Elizabeth. It may have been a difficult journey, but Mary did not wait for an opportune time. This may show an impulsive side or just the zeal to talk with Elizabeth!*
- *She was the kind of guest that could stay for 3 months. It is rare to have outsiders that fit with your household well enough to share such an extended time.*
- *Mary's prayer of praise shows her heart, which is amazing.*

**Reflections on Mary back to Nazareth**

1. How would you feel if the girl you were to marry tells you she is pregnant miraculously?

*I suspect most would not continue with the marriage and would want it publicly known why they broke it off. You would want others to know the child was not yours.*

2. What did Mary face as a single pregnant girl?

*She could have faced stoning under the law for being pregnant while betrothed (Deuteronomy 22:23–24). Mary lived in a small community, where there would be gossip and possibly shunning of someone who broke the law in a small community.*

3. Describe what Joseph and Mary's relationship would have been for the six months before going to Bethlehem?
*There was probably a wedding; it is not clear when. The wedding party would have been for a week or so (John 2:2-5). The custom was a parade through the streets from Mary's house to Joseph's home. According to traditions, the bride would indicate her virginity by going with her hair unbound (unbraided).*
*After the wedding, they didn't have the usual honeymoon. I hope they developed a friendship as people who have been given a*

*shared mission. (I hear the Mission Impossible music in the background.)*

## Reflections on Mary to Bethlehem

1. Luke 2:1-5 explains Joseph went to Bethlehem to register for the census, but why did a very pregnant Mary go with him?

*It is not clear why. Since they stayed in Bethlehem after Jesus's birth, it is possible that they had decided to move to Bethlehem and Mary was coming with Joseph to relocate. They may have wanted to leave the gossip in Nazareth. When returning from Egypt, it seems Joseph initially was headed back to Judah (possibly Bethlehem, Matthew 2:22), but after being warned in a dream again, detoured to Galilee and back to Mary's home of Nazareth.*

2. Mary treasured what the shepherds shared in her heart (Luke 2:19). What were the points from the shepherd's story you would put in your child's scrapbook?

*In 1 Peter 1:12 it mentions that angels longed to see the good news! The heavenly host were so excited about His birth that they had to tell someone! The shepherds would tell Mary that a heavenly hosts came giving glory to God and telling them that the Savior and Christ was in a manger. Mary would appreciate their hurry to see even if she was exhausted and put all this in her scrapbook.*

## Reflections on Mary at the Temple

1. Mary and Joseph follow Moses' law and offer doves as a sacrifice for their firstborn. Most assume it indicates a family that is not wealthy enough to have a lamb to offer. What would be the pros and cons for Jesus to be raised n a wealthy or frugal home?
*A wealthy family would be able to provide education, resources and religious training. They would have social connections. Jesus would not have to work or have any physical hardships. He could focus on his ministry and work change from the inside of the power structure.*
*Would HE really need any of that? Would the Pharisees and Sadducees listen and change if Jesus had been from their group? Not likely.*

*Growing up with six (maybe more) siblings in a small town with limited resources helped Jesus experience the many challenges we face. He understands our struggles.*

2. How would you expect Mary to react after her day at the Temple with Jesus?

*Mary, likely overwhelmed with joy at the public recognition of her son as the Messiah by Simeon and Anna, was also cautioned to expect hardship and opposition. Simeon tempered her joy with the reality of future suffering.*

**Reflections on Mary lives in Bethlehem**

1. What do the actions of the wise men suggest about their relationship with God?

*The wise men knew of the Messiah and sought to worship Him. This is not a short trip, but a major commitment. They brought expensive gifts that I would be concerned about carrying over the road. They were provided with a star to follow and were told in a dream to avoid Herod. They showed a knowledge and understanding of God and He took care of them. While Simeon spoke of Gentiles being included. These were the first Gentiles who worshipped Jesus.*

2. In Acts 10:28 Peter expresses his concern about associating or visiting a Gentile with Cornelius. This suggest that first century devout Jews would be resistant to share a meal or entertain Gentiles in their homes. In Galatians 2:11-14 Paul addresses Peter's continued resistance, although he finally overcame his bias. How did Mary react to Gentiles (the wise men) coming into her home?
*Mary was probably shocked and surprised. Since the wise men's story indicates a strong relationship with Jehovah it would be difficult to shun what God has supported (Acts 11:17-18 shares the Jewish Christian's reaction to Corneilius's story). It is also difficult to turn away people who give you something (That is why car dealerships want to 'give' you something first.) Mary invited them into her home and heard about their journey to see the King.*

*Mary may have felt amazed and blessed to see people from distant lands honoring her son. It affirmed her faith, though she would soon face trials.*

### Reflections on Mary lives in Egypt

1. How might Egypt have influenced Mary's understanding of Simeon's warning?

*The flight to Egypt and the need to hide may have deepened her awareness that Jesus would face opposition and danger. Although the initial danger was from Herod, she would see where the real danger would be.*

### Reflections on Mary settles back in Nazareth

1. What was life in Nazareth like for Mary and Joseph?

*They returned to Galilee and lived a normal family life—working, raising children, attending synagogue, keeping the sabbath, and traveling annually to Jerusalem for Passover.*

2. What do you think were the challenges and benefits of having Jesus and several siblings?

*Oh my, raising a perfect child such as Jesus alongside ordinary children may have caused parenting difficulties, including perceptions of favoritism. As the oldest, Jesus would have helped with the other children and later left to work with Joseph. He would have experience of a small house with seven (maybe more) children.*

3. How has Mary learned to depend to God?

*Let's review Mary's first few years:*

- *Mary's expectations of a normal life were dashed by Gabriel's message.*
- *She went to Elizabeth for information and a tutorial on letting God lead and basking in their understanding that her son was the Messiah.*
- *She told Joseph about her pregnancy - he didn't believe her until God told him in a dream.*

- *Others probably didn't believe her conception story either. However, the shepherds told her – Jesus was King, Simeon told her, Anna told her, and Gentiles traveled a long way to show her Jesus was the King. When Mary fled to Egypt to save Jesus, they had resources to live on. They returned to danger and hid in Nazareth.*

*Mary had a turbulent first few years of marriage – away from family, but God always gave her the physical and spiritual support she needed.*

*Mary's struggles led her to depend on God.*

4. What are some of Mary's strengths that we can emulate?

*There are many, this is only the beginning of this discussion. Mary was calm, practical, willing to experience change, kind to Gentiles (others outside her clique), protective, a scrapbooker (when she puts things in her heart that's what I think of), knowledgeable of God, reverent, humble, and excited by the Good News!*

*Mary had the kind of faith, and trust in God that didn't say – 'wait, let me think about it' but said yes, as a servant of the Lord.*

5. What weaknesses did Mary show that we should be aware of in ourselves?

*When Jesus was not with them to return to Nazareth, Mary forgot whose son Jesus was. That is something to remember. Jesus was God who took on physical form (John 1:1, 14, Colossians 2:9, Philippians 2:6-8, Hebrews 1:3, and John 10:30-33.) She assumed He would do what she thought He should. Jesus reminded her whose son He was.*

## Reflection on Anna

1. If you went to the temple and saw Anna, what would you think?

*Initially, maybe she was odd. Why spend your life praying for a Redeemer that God will send in his own time. It is easy to dismiss something when we don't understand. Eventually, I hope to respect her passion. If I needed a prayer, I would ask her to pray. She would become someone to admire and respect. Someone that I relied on for her dedication. She would become a rock when going to the temple. Someone I knew would be there praying. Anna is not the flashy prophet, but the quiet tower of strength to look forward to seeing.*

2. What did Anna not do?

*She didn't give up. Sometimes it is difficult to stay focused during prayer, she didn't lose her motivation.*
*She didn't stop because she was old. To age well we should eat healthily (don't overeat), stay active, be socially engaged and have a passion. Anna did it all and saw the Redeemer!*
*She didn't forget to thank God. We pray for God's help, then when the prayer is answered, we forget to thank Him. Thankfulness was the first words from Anna when she saw Jesus.*
*She didn't take casseroles to the sick. Well, maybe she did, but she may have had limited resources, so she did what she could, prayed and fasted at the temple.*

3. Describe what you feel are Anna's strengths?

- *Five decades of prayer, fasting and worship indicate a level of perseverance and discipline that is impressive.*
- *Spiritual focus on seeking the Redeemer. She did not swerve in what she sought.*
- *She is called a prophet and recognized Jesus immediately (discernment).*
- *Thankfulness. Anna immediately gave thanks when God answered her prayers. She didn't forget that all was from God.*
- *It takes courage to publicly witnessed that Jesus was the Redeemer.*
- *As a widow, she was vulnerable socially, but she focused on God for decades.*

4. What were some possible limitations for Anna?

- *Since many encourage widows to remarry, Anna dismissed cultural norms. Others may have marginalized her for not conforming.*
- *She may have been lonely in her solitary service.*

## Reflections on Mary at the wedding

1. What does Mary's response to the servants, "Do whatever He tells you", tell us about her understanding of Jesus?

*Mary's words reveal deep trust and confidence in Jesus. She didn't demand or explain—she simply believed He would act rightly. Her instruction to the servants shows that she understood Jesus' authority and wisdom, even if she didn't know exactly how He would respond. It reflects her spiritual insight and maternal faith — she knew His heart.*

2. What are some possible reasons Mary knew Jesus would help?

*Mary had lived with Jesus for thirty years. She knew His character, His kindness, wisdom, and sense of responsibility. She may have witnessed countless quiet acts of compassion in the home or community. She also knew the promises spoken to her before His birth. Mary was appealing to the one she believed capable of making things right. She had spent 30 years with Him. She likely believed that He would help, even if the timing wasn't ideal.*

3. What lessons can we learn from Mary's example when we encounter a need or a problem? How can we imitate her posture of faith and her simple direction: "Do whatever He tells you"?

*Mary brings the problem to Jesus, not with panic but with confidence. She doesn't try to control the outcome. Mary didn't tell Jesus what to do. She brought the issue to his attention, then she simply trusts that He will act in the right way. Her example teaches us to take our concerns to the Lord, then step back and trust. "Do whatever He tells you", is a beautiful model for discipleship. When we're uncertain, the safest path is always to listen to His instruction and obey it.*

4. How did Jesus honor his mother (Exodus 20:12, Deuteronomy 5:16, Matthew 15:3-6, Mark 7:9-13, Matthew 19:17-19, Mark 10:19: Luke 18:20**).**

*Jesus was obedient to his parents, Luke 2:51.*
*At the wedding in Cana, Mary tells Jesus, "They have no wine." Though He responds, "My hour has not yet come," Jesus honors*

*her concern and performs a public miracle, turning water into wine. His actions suggest a willingness to respect her request, even as He responds that He is not ready to share His identity publicly yet.*

### Reflections on the Samaritan Woman

1. When others believed because of her testimony about Jesus, what does that imply about the Samaritan woman?

*Her testimony was believed and trusted. She was not someone who lied easily. She may have had social issues, but people believed her testimony. What characteristics are in those you trust and believe?*

2. If we assume it was not a coincidence that Jesus was alone by the well when the woman came (or Jesus knew she would be there and sent his followers away). Why would Jesus seek her out?

*Jesus knows men's hearts. He knew she was honest, had a rough life (5 husbands?) and was interested in spiritual discussions. Jesus is a shepherd seeking the lost, and the woman was seeking the Messiah. This is a great example of how those seeking find in unexpected ways.*

3. What are some strengths from this woman we should emulate?

- *She was honest, practical, interested in spiritual discussions, respectful, and seized the opportunity to talk with a prophet.*
- *Others respected and believed her, or they would not have come to see Jesus and believe Him because of her testimony.*

4. Are there weaknesses we should recognize to avoid?

- She seemed to have some religious bias.
- Five husbands is probably not a good track record in maintaining relationships.

## Reflections on Peter's mother-in-law

1. What are we to learn from this story about Peter's mother-in-law?

*She was cherished. There was concern by many when she was sick. The concern expressed by others indicates that she was loved.*

*It seems she was a widow. While widows are frequently taken care of by sons, This is an example of a widow staying with her daughter's family.*

*Peter's mother-in-law teaches us a simple lesson: when Jesus heals and restores us, our natural response should be service. Her immediate action, getting up to serve, shows gratitude coupled with action. We don't have a record of her voicing her appreciation, but she showed her thoughts through her works.*

## Reflections on the Widow of Nain

1. Why would this widow be the one Jesus helped?

- She was a widow with no other children (the word interpreted son in some versions, also means child), likely without economic means or social protection. In that society, she would have been vulnerable and alone, without support.
- Jesus was moved by compassion. His presence was not requested. He saw her pain and acted. If it wasn't a coincidence, Jesus walked for 8+ hours to be there and help this widow.
- Luke shares a story of Peter going to a town to raise Tabitha from the dead (Acts 9:36-42). Tabitha was someone who had worked to help others. Maybe this widow was also one to show benevolence, but there is no scripture on her background.
- This miracle gave a public stage for Jesus to reveal His power over death and His deep compassion, which caused the people to glorify God and proclaim that God's presence had returned to His people through Jesus.

2. We don't have the widow's reaction or much about her. We only have how the people supported her and Jesus's actions. Do you see any strength to remember?

*The number of people that were there for her indicates someone appreciated and respected by many. Jesus knows our hearts. The implication is that she was someone Jesus cared for and wanted to help.*

### Reflections on the Weeping Sinner

1. What do you think was the woman's plan when she went to Simon's house?

*She likely came with the intention of honoring Jesus by anointing Him with perfume, a sign of respect and devotion. She might have heard Jesus teach before or what He taught and wanted to participate. Her original plan may have been quiet and reverent, but she was overcome by emotion, and her response became more personal and spontaneous, marked by tears, humility, and repentance.*
*She is an example of someone who sought mercy and found it. (Matthew 7:7)*

2. What are some strengths we could learn from this sinner?

- *Humility: She didn't defend herself or hide; she came openly and broken.*
- *Courage: She entered a Pharisee's home, knowing the judgment she would face.*
- *Love: She gave what she had, poured out emotionally and materially.*
- *Repentance: She acknowledged her need for grace through action, not words.*
- *Faith: She believed that Jesus had the authority to forgive and heal her life.*
- *Discernment: Recognized the source of peace.*

### Reflections on The Toucher

1. What are some of the limitations that chronic illness brings?

*Weakness, tiredness, depression, financial costs, depression and emotional isolation. Not things that increase interest in going out into a crowd.*

*If you are studying with a group, those who deal with chronic conditions could share some of their struggles. How do chronic conditions compare with short-term ailments/injuries?*

2. When Jesus turns and confronts the woman, the crowd probably goes silent. What strength did the woman use to answer Jesus?

*She conquered her fear and weakness. Embarrassment at someone 'unclean' touching a prophet might have been a concern.*

3. What are the woman's strengths?

*Honesty to tell the truth in front of a crowd. She was trembling, so probably afraid, but she conquered her fear. Took a chance that she would be able to get close enough to touch and had faith that Jesus had power so great that proximity was all she needed.*

*She sought help (Matthew 7:7). She had heard of Jesus and had faith that he could help her.*

## Reflections on Herodias and Salome

1. What seems to have motivated Herodias in her actions toward John the Baptist and her marriage decisions?

*Herodias was originally married to Herod II, a potential heir to Herod the Great. However, when Herod II was disinherited, he lost his political future and likely much of his wealth. Living quietly in Rome, he held no territory and had little power. Herodias may have desired a return to political influence, wealth, and visibility—things Herod Antipas, ruler of Galilee and Perea, could offer. She could also have had feelings for him; the verses do not share her full motivation.*

*By leaving Herod II and marrying Herod Antipas, Herodias elevated her status and income, aligning herself with a reigning tetrarch. However, John the Baptist's public condemnation of their marriage threatened her position and reputation. According to Mark 6:19, Herodias held a grudge against John, and she was probably aware of Antipas's interest in John.*

*Her actions indicated her fear that Herod Antipas might listen to John, and she would lose everything she controlled.*

2. Was Salome a pawn in Herodias's scheme or did she have a choice?

*According to Mark 6:24, after Herod Antipas promised to grant her any request, Salome immediately went to her mother for direction, asking, "What shall I ask for?" This suggests she did not have her own agenda and was guided, or perhaps manipulated, by Herodias.*

*If Salome knew her mother well, and she likely did, she may have been aware of Herodias's intense desire to see John silenced. Perhaps she anticipated the request and chose to carry it out without question. On the other hand, she could have resisted. Ultimately, Salome followed her mother's instructions precisely, though it's notable that she adds the addition of a platter to place the head as presentation. Nevertheless, she delivered the gruesome request, a decision that would define her legacy. It is a tragic moment: a young woman remembered throughout history for participating in the death of John the Baptist.*

3. What are Herodias's strengths?

*Herodias appears to have been intelligent, politically astute, and determined. She understood how power worked within the Herodian dynasty and positioned herself to regain influence after her first husband, Herod II, was disinherited. It's possible that she seized the opportunity to elevate her status by marrying Herod Antipas. It is unknown if she had feelings for Herod Antipas or was attracted to his position and power. If her action was based on feelings, I would think she would be concerned with Herod's fear about killing a prophet, as it was an action that haunted Herod Antipas. (Matthew 14:1-2, Mark 6:14-16, Luke 9:7-9).*

*Herodias exhibited persistence (in a bad way). She carried a long-standing grudge against John the Baptist and waited for the right moment to act. Her ability to influence people, especially her daughter and husband, shows she possessed strong persuasive skills and a sharp understanding of social dynamics.*

4. Herodias was a murderer. While we don't act to the extent she did, what are her weaknesses that we also struggle to control?

*Herodias was vindictive and morally blind. She allowed personal offense and fear to override justice and righteousness. Instead of confronting John's criticism with humility or repentance or ignoring it, she harbored a grudge. She didn't want to change her position. Was it pride or feelings for Herod Antipas? Her actions suggest a willingness to manipulate others, including her own daughter, to protect her position.*

*Herodias was willing to include her daughter in the murder of John. Not someone who seemed to care about her daughter's spirit.*

5. Ultimately, Salome's actions define her character. What are her strengths and weaknesses?

*Salome's strengths are difficult to identify, but she demonstrated dancing skill, and obedience. She showed loyalty to her mother by seeking her advice, when she could have asked for her own reward, and carrying out her wishes without hesitation.*

*However, her weaknesses include a lack of moral discernment and personal agency. Whether due to youth, fear, or blind obedience, she participated in a gruesome act without apparent question or protest. Her readiness to deliver such a request suggests that either she did not fully grasp the gravity of her actions, she lacked the strength to stand up against wrongdoing, or she supported killing John to secure her position. Her legacy is tragically tied to a moment in which she followed orders instead of doing the right action.*

If you would like to view some of the paintings depicting this event, search for:

- Salome with the Head of John the Baptist" and "The Beheading of Saint John the Baptist" – Caravaggio (c. 1607–1610)
- "Salome with the Head of John the Baptist" – Titian (c. 1515)
- "Salome with the Head of John the Baptist" – Bernardino Luini (c. 1527)
- "Salome" – Franz von Stuck (1906)
- "Salome with the Head of John the Baptist" – Peter Paul Rubens (c. 1609)

## Reflections on the Canaanite Woman

1. If the Canaanite had been insulted by Jesus's analogy to dogs, what would she have done?

*She may have walked away in anger, bitterness, or despair, missing the opportunity for her daughter's healing. Her humility, persistence, and quick response provided an opportunity for mercy to Gentiles.*

a. Do we every get insulted and walk away from an opportunity to glorify God?

*Probably more than we think.*

2. This Canaanite and the centurion both had faith that Jesus's words alone would 'make it so'. Were there other commonalities?

*They were both Gentiles who believed Jesus. It is not sure if they also worshipped idols, but they understood that Jesus had power their idols did not.*

3.What are some negotiation skills the Phoenician used?

a. Set a clear goal.
b. Be respectful of the other party's restrictions.
c. Recognize the other party's power and choices.
d. Reframe objections.
e. Begin with a 'low cost' agreement.
f. Ask for agreement and close.

4. What are the strengths of this Phoenician woman?

- *Humility: She accepted her position as an outsider, even embracing Jesus's analogy as dogs.*
- *Faith: Despite being a Gentile, she recognized Jesus's power and authority, believing He could heal her daughter with just a word.*
- *Perseverance: She didn't give up when initially refused but pressed on with respectful determination.*
- *Discernment: She grasped the heart of Jesus's message and responded with wisdom, showing spiritual insight beyond cultural and religious boundaries.*
- *Respectful: she responded with humility, acknowledging His greater position.*
- *Good negotiator and diplomate.*
- *Courageous: It is easier to do nothing. She sought out Jesus and approached Him, when others were trying to keep her away.*
- *Loving. She was motivated by love for her daughter*
- *She is another who sought help (Matthew 7:7).*

## Reflections on Mary Magdalene, Joanna, Susanna and others

1. How do you think the women helped during Jesus's work?

*They may have helped with meals, cared for the group's daily needs, offered hospitality in various towns, and managed travel logistics. Packing, washing, cleaning, networking to find the best place to stay. They may have networked their friends as family as Jesus traveled. Their financial support would let Jesus focus on teaching.*
*Women were not included as disciples by Rabbis during this period, so it is significant that Jesus taught the women and they traveled with the group.*

2. To leave your home and travel with Jesus and a group of men would take quite a commitment. What strengths allowed these women to support Jesus in his work?

*Travel requires organization and resourcefulness. It would not be a comfortable trip, with walking, cleaning, carrying supplies, etc. They would need to be flexible and physically fit. Work at home*

*probably didn't stop, so they needed a network to keep things functioning.*
*There were a lot of people healed and received help from Jesus, but only a few actually dropped their lives to spend time with Him. This took discernment to recognize Jesus. A desire to help Him help others, faith and love to see the greater value.*

3. If women were not allowed in the schools and had separate spaces in synagogues and the temple, how would Jesus's inclusion of the women with his disciples challenge norms?

*This would have been a recognition of women's understanding of scriptures and their involvement in his ministry.*

## Reflections on the Adulterer

1. Why do you think she stayed when all her accusers had left? Why not run?

*Scared to leave or realized Jesus's wisdom and power? Her respectful response suggests she recognized Jesus was different.*

2. There was a show that put minor offenders in with criminals, so the minor offenders would be 'scared straight'. A moment of clarity where the outcome of your choices becomes undeniable. We don't know the outcome, but the adulterer had an experience that would be difficult to forget. What would it take for you to be 'scared straight' from your secret sin?

*For some it might be the public knowledge or a self-revelation of a secret sin in a way that could not be ignored. It might be realizing the hurt caused to others, feeling the shame, or how it has distanced them from God. Ultimately, Jesus shows the grace and mercy that is waiting if we will change.*

## Reflections on Blind Man's Mother

All the responses are from both parents,
1. If someone healed your child from a debilitating illness, what would keep you from telling everyone the good news?

*If the benefactor asked to remain anonymous or it wasn't available to anyone else.*

*The parents seem more concerned with punishment from spiritual leaders than the joy of knowing their son could see!*

2. What weakness do you think the mother of the Blind Man struggles?

*Not willing to put themselves at risk. Ruled by fear of spiritual leaders. Possibly more concerned about what could happen to her than what happened to her child.*

*Does she recognize and realize the power of God (Mark 12:24)?*

### Reflections on Mary and Martha Part 1

1. Did Martha need the same spiritual food as Mary?

*There are several ways we feed our spirit. Singing, praying, seeing His hand in creation, and listening to His words. We have different needs and many ways to grow spiritually. While missing an opportunity to listen directly to Jesus seems like a poor choice; Martha shows her faith.*

*There is a book, The Five Love Languages by Dr. Gary Chapman that talks about how we have different ways of showing love. I think of Martha as the one who shows love with Acts of Service. Mary may be the one who needs Quality Time.*

2. What does Jesus's defense of Mary's right to learn alongside the male disciples, rather than being separated or confined to serving, reveal about His view of women's roles?

*Jesus did not expect women to serve, while the men learn. Jesus challenged cultural norms that limited women's spiritual participation. He recognized women as worthy of theological instruction and placed spiritual growth above traditional expectations.*

3. It is easy to choose sides, Mary or Martha. What are the joys of being "a Mary?" Is there also pleasure in serving like Martha?

*Mary has the joy of hearing God with ALL her senses! We read and talk to others about God, but Mary could absorb with ears, sight, touch and even smell. Something most women would not have been allowed.*
*Martha had the joy of serving God!*

## Reflections on Blessing Woman

1. Does it matter what we bless?

*Jesus gently corrects the woman regarding her blessing and redirects her blessing. There are several passages that guide our blessings: Luke 6:28 suggests we should bless those who curse us. Romans 12:14 says to bless those who persecute you. Psalms 115:13; 128:1-2 tells us that God blesses those who fear the Lord and walk in his ways. And we should bless the Lord (Psalms 103:1-2, 34:1).*
*Compare Jesus's correction of this woman and His correction for the Scribes and Pharisees.*

2. What is the weakness of the Blessing woman?

*She focused on physical family and ignored the greater value of our spiritual family.*

## Reflections on Bent Woman

1. How might living with a long-term illness affect someone's relationship with God?

*Chronic illness can challenge a person's faith and those that help care for the person. It makes us question God, incites frustration and even doubt.*

*It can also deepen our dependence on God, change our perspective and increase empathy for others. The Bent Woman's presence at the synagogue suggests she had not given up on God. Her faith endured.*

2. Luck is what happens when preparation meets opportunity'. Seneca, Roman philosopher. This reflects the idea that being in the right place, doing the right thing, positions someone when the

moment arrives. Did the woman 'get lucky' or does her healing reflect her faithful presence in worship?

*We don't know her habits, but her attendance and Jesus's call to her suggests that she was there without any expectation of healing. If it was her practice, it says a lot about her interest in God and God's concern for her.*

3. What would you suggest are the Bent woman's strengths?

*Persistent faith in the face of chronic illness. It is easy to stay home with chronic illness and avoid other. But we need the social contact and encouragement of other disciples. She made the effort to go to worship even when it was a struggle.*

### Reflections on Mary and Martha Part 2

1. Why would Martha, Mary and the others expect Jesus to keep Lazarus from dying?

*Jesus loved them, had a relationship with them and He had the power to help.*

2. From Martha's declaration in John 11:27 what do we know about her developing faith?

*Martha knew Jesus was a prophet, and she believed in the resurrection. At Lazarus's grave she realized Jesus was the Son of God. Her faith went from doctrine (belief in the resurrection) to God the person (belief in Jesus).*

### Reflections on the Mother of James and John

1. What characteristic would Salome have to make this request of Jesus?

*She was interested in securing power for her sons. She didn't understand that the kingdom was not physical. After Jesus's refusal, she continued to stay, showing loyalty and persistence.*

2. Why would Salome continue to support Jesus even as her request is denied?

*She may have realized what Peter did in John 6:68 when Jesus asked if he would leave as other disciples had left. 'Lord, to whom shall we go? You have the words of eternal life.'*

### Reflections on Mary and Martha Part 3

1. Are you surprised that Martha is serving?

*No, that is Martha's nature. She is the one helping others. Even at Simon's house, Martha is organizing and taking care of service.*

2. Jesus prophesies that Mary would be remember for her work. Did that happen?

*Yes, we are still talking about her act of honor.*

3. Jesus defends Mary again. What was Mary doing this time that Jesus defended (Luke 10:39, John 12:3)?

*Initially Jesus defended Mary for listening to Him instead of helping. And the second time He defended her for honoring Him.*

Our first interaction with Mary and Martha focuses on their exchange with Jesus. The second shared Martha's faith at the raising of Lazarus. The last story showed Mary's understanding of Jesus's mission. Over the three events of Mary and Martha in Part 1, 2 and 3 consider:

4. How would you describe Martha's strengths?

*Martha was practical, calm, loyal and a servant. She didn't hold a grudge when Jesus told her to leave Mary alone or when He didn't come to heal Lazarus. She displayed faith that Jesus had the power to heal and save.*

*Martha sends for Jesus, meets Jesus and acknowledges He is the Messiah. If you need help, Martha is the one you would call.*

5. What are Mary's strengths?

*Mary put a priority on spiritual. She seems to be emotional, loving and someone who wants to learn.*

*Mary consistently did actions that Jesus defended. Doing action that Jesus defends is something that we should all want. She prioritized listening to Jesus and honoring Him.*

## Reflections on the Giving Widow

1. What does the widow teach us about generosity and dependence on God?

*Generosity is measured on sacrifice, not by the monetary amount. God sees our generosity based on our ability. Not on monetary value.*

*God sees those who depend on Him with faith. I believe after the widow gave all she had; there was food to eat and a place to stay for her. To make the offering of all her funds, she must have learned to depend on God (See Matthew 6:25-34). She shows me how far I need to go to really have trust in God.*

## Reflection on the Servant woman

1. Why would she care if Jesus's disciple was in the courtyard?

*Jesus was treated as a criminal, and she might have been concerned that his friends would try to free him.*

## Reflections on Pilate's wife

1. Why would Pilate's wife care if her husband ruled against Jesus?

*She was told in a dream that Jesus was righteous and warned Pilate not to get involved. It is not clear whether she was concerned with justice or limiting her husband's involvement in an injustice.*

## Reflections on Women at the Cross

1. Why would these women choose to be with Jesus throughout his suffering and death?

*Love, loyalty, compassion, or too shocked to do anything else? James and John's mother expected a physical kingdom (Matthew 20:20-21). Were the others expecting Jesus to become the King of*

*Judea? They had to be in shock. Jesus who had controlled everything, taken and killed.*

*The women may have chosen to comfort the suffering. I suspect there was disbelief, prayer, and hope Jesus would step off the cross at any moment.*

*There may have been advantages to be a woman at the cross. Guards may have dispersed groups of men as a potential threat, whereas women were not intimidating. There are times when being ignored is helpful. This might have been such an event. We don't know their thoughts during Jesus's time at the cross, but we know they were there.*

2. Why would others choose to avoid watching Jesus die?

*Jesus prepped the disciples in several ways. He sent the apostles out on their own and a group of disciples to train them to work without Him (Mark 6:7-13, Matthew 10:1-15, Luke 9:1-6, Luke 10:1-20). He told them He would be taken and killed, but it didn't 'sink-in'. Even in this last week, they expected Jesus to be King, and they would be His cabinet (Matthew 20: 22-28). Without Jesus, they didn't know what to do.*

*It's possible the disciples expected guards to keep them away from Jesus. The men followers might have been intentionally excluded from the area as potential anarchists. It does not say.*

3. Once Jesus was in the tomb, what did the women do?

*Stayed busy. It seems like everyone has a shroud or burial stuff available 'just in case'. Josephus supplied the initial material, but the women went back to gather the rest to use after the Passover Yom Tov and Sabbath.*

*They would have coordinated what to take and when to be at the tomb, daylight. They were not from Jerusalem, but Galilee. They may be staying at different locations. If some stayed in Bethany, they would prepare for the early morning walk to the tomb. Others might be staying in Jerusalem.*

*They prepped for the Sabbath and followed the law, resting and focusing on God. It had to be a tough Sabbath to honor.*

4. What are some ways to deal with grief?

*Staying busy and serving others. Share your sorrow. Give thanks and remember the joy. What are your suggestions?*

**Reflections on Mary at the Cross Part 3**

1. When Jesus entrusted Mary to John's care, He separated her from her biological sons and daughters. How would Mary have felt being told to leave her sons and possible grandchildren to stay with John?

*Her immediate response was the same as when Gabriel told her she would have a miraculous birth – obedience. She moved in with John. In doing so, Mary lived out what Jesus had taught in Matthew 12:48–50, embracing her spiritual family as her true family. Mary might have been unhappy leaving her sons and daughters, but John may have needed some of her strengths. Mary continued to be the obedient, maidservant of the Lord.*

*It is possible that John's mother was also the woman called Salome, who is mentioned as Mary's sister. It there is a family connection, then John would be Mary's nephew (Jesus's cousin). This might have kept Mary close to her children and grandchildren.*

2. How would Mary be able to help John?

*Mary's presence could have deepened John's understanding of Christ's life and mission in ways that few others could experience firsthand. Jesus gave John the gift of living alongside an example of faith. Mary had been with Jesus longer than any other person.*

*Mary's life reflected faithfulness that endured through joy and sorrow, courage that stood unshaken at the cross, humility that embraced God's will, devotion that followed Jesus to the end, prayerfulness that waited for the Spirit, and a direct witness to the humanity of Christ. Traits echoed in John's writings: the Word made flesh, abiding in Christ, loving one another, walking in truth, and fear not, for perfect love casts out fear. These are not John's abstract ideas; they are lessons seen in Mary.*

*It is notable that Scripture never records John having a wife or children. Traditions suggest that John lived a long, single life ministering in Ephesus and later exiled to Patmos. And Mary would have been with him as long as she lived.*

### Reflections on Women at the Tomb

1. Jesus teaches several times that those who are first will be last, and the last will be first - Mark 10:28-31& Matthew 19:30 (left everything), Mark 9:33-37 & Luke 14:8-11 (humble), Matthew 20:1-28 (service). The women from Galilee, not the apostles or Pharisee or rulers, were the first to hear the good news, the first to see, and the first to touch Jesus. How does this exemplify Jesus's teachings on reversals?

*It is a great of example of Jesus actions matching his teaching. These women left Galilee and supported Jesus's work. They served and were first to see Jesus and hear He had risen. News that people had waited centuries to hear. The last were first.*

2. The women from Galilee are mentioned by Luke early in Jesus's work (Luke 8:1-3). Reflect on their efforts and time with Jesus, particularly as they stood vigil at Jesus death and came to complete his burial. What were their strengths we should copy?

*They were generous with funds, time and efforts. The women were brave to remain where others are berating and abusing Jesus. They were organized, hard-working (imagine standing at the cross, then returning home to prepare for Jesus's burial and the Sabbath), kind, helpful, obedient, faithful. Persistent – they were the disciples who stayed with Jesus to the end. Joyful – can you feel Mary Magdalene's joy when she recognized Jesus!*

3. What are the weaknesses over the last few days of Jesus's life that we should watch in ourselves?

*Mark mentions that after a messenger tells the women Jesus has risen some fled the tomb. They were trembling and afraid and did not share the news that Jesus had risen (Mark 16:8). Since other writers say that the women told others that Jesus was alive, it seems that possibly some were so afraid they did not share the news; or they were afraid initially and later told others. Fear is a reason we do not always share the news about Jesus. We are afraid of what others might think or say. We are afraid we won't glorify God, so we don't try.*

## Reflection on Sapphira

1. What would happen if people were struck dead when they intentionally mislead others?

*People would be careful not to mislead or there would be fewer people. We would know people would tell the truth.*

2. Can you think of an example of when truth is secondary to keeping up appearances?

*Unfortunately, abuse in family may be hid by lies. People may believe abuse is their fault, or they are embarrassed and hide it or pretend there is not a problem.*
*What are some other examples?*

3. What do you think was Sapphira's strength?

*She chooses to follow Jesus's teaching and was part of the early church when Christians were being persecuted.*

4. What was Sapphira's weakness?

*She apparently thought supporting deception was more important than telling the truth. If she had said she would not lie about the amount, it may have stopped the lie early. When leadership is unrighteous, it shouldn't be followed.*

## Reflection of Hellenistic women

1. Why are people who don't speak the local language, or in the same group easy to overlook?

*It takes more time and effort to reach out to those who are different.*

## Reflections on women in prison

1. If you are thrown in prison for your belief, does it make a difference if your spouse or mother is also put in prison?

*There is a protective instinct and seeing those you should protect being abused would be especially difficult.*

2. What are the strengths of the women and men who went to prison because they believed in Jesus?

*Courage and they see the long-term goal. It is difficult for many to see beyond the current need, desire or want. Christians see that eternal life with Jesus is worth persecutions.*

## Reflections on Tabitha

1. What changes within the family, when that person (male or female) died or was no longer able to be the 'glue' for the group?

*Families may lose a sense of connection when the organizer dies. Gatherings and traditions fade, and a void may develop unless others take responsibility.*

2. There is some evidence that helping others is a tool to reduce stress. If true, would you expect Tabitha to be stressed? How would you describe her?

*Those who serve from compassion often experience joy and fulfillment, not anxiety, because their focus is outward rather than inward. I would expect Tabitha to be busy but probably didn't have high blood pressure!*

## Reflections on Mary and Rhoda

1. What strengths would Mary have to host Christians during this time?

*She would have been generous with her home: hospitable. When Christians are being taken to prison, she would also be brave and hopefully good at keeping the Christian location a secret.*

2. Rhoda makes me smile, why would it be good to be like Rhoda?

*Her enthusiasm and joy that Peter was free are wonderful to see. She was probably frustrated, no one believed her, but she could have opened the door!*

## Reflections on Devout and Prominent Women

1. What were the strengths and possible weaknesses of these devout and prominent women?

*From the effect it seems the women had political power and were influenced by the Jewish leaders against Paul and Barnabas.*

## Reflections on Lois and Eunice

1. What is the value of Lois's faith?

*Lois's faith is a spiritual inheritance. She created the foundation for two generations. While Lois is not described as a teacher, leader, or missionary, her quiet faith had ripple effects that reached far beyond her own life. By nurturing Eunice and Timothy, she indirectly shaped Paul's ministry partner and, through Timothy, the churches of Ephesus, Corinth, Philippi, and others.*

*Lois is a reminder that many Christians have an effect on others they may not see directly.*

2. What skills or traits would have helped Lois and Eunice share their faith with Timothy?

- *Knowledge of scriptures: 2 Timothy 3:15 suggest Lois and Eunice were intentional in teaching the Bible to Timothy.*
- *Consistency and Sincerity: Timothy would see genuine devotion lived out daily.*
- *Perseverance under pressure: As Jewish Christians, they likely faced opposition from the Jewish community in Derbe. But they remained steadfast, modeling courage and commitment to Timothy. It may have been helpful under these conditions to have a Gentile husband, son-in-low and father.*

- *Nurturing: Traits of patience, tenderness, and encouragement would have created an environment where faith could take root.*

### Reflection on Lydia and women of Philippi

1. What does it indicate when your household follows your lead?

*It seems Lydia was someone that her family and servants respected enough to follow her lead. Leaders have a greater responsibility (James 3:1). They can lead people in a positive way or down a path that is harmful. Lydia led her household to hear and believe in Jesus.*

2. How would you describe Lydia's strengths?
*Lydia was the kind of person that her household followed. She was hospitable, kind and prayerful. She would meet with other women routinely to pray. She was part of the church that was close to Paul and repeatedly supported his teaching.*

### Reflections on the Leading women of Thessalonica and Berea

1. How would Paul and Silas talk to leading Greek women?

*The prominent or leading women were probably educated and wealthy. They may have participated in public duties as 'Patrons' and been at public forums (Gardner, page 264). Paul may have talked to Jewish women at the synagogue or in homes. They would not have been by themselves, but with escorts.*

### Reflections on Damaris

1. What were challenges that Damaris would have as a new Christian in Athens?

*Learning more about Jesus and finding other Christians to meet with would have been a challenge. Women in Athens would have participated in rituals, songs and processions for the festival of Demeter and Persephone (only women would have participated), Panathenaea (festival for Athena), Eleusinian mysteries initiations. Leaving the participation in familiar rituals is difficult. Damaris would need internal strength to follow Jesus.*

## Reflections on Priscilla

1. What is the benefit of a strong wife and husband team in teaching the Gospel?

*Each has different strengths and perspectives. Working with others when we have complementary skills makes a team stronger. Their record of service indicates a very supportive and skilled couple.*

2. How could Priscilla and Aquilla have risked their lives for Paul?

*There were riots and threats to Paul on multiple occasions. Being a close companion, they probably were in a position to protect him, while risking themselves.*

3. Does the order of names with Priscilla and Aquilla indicate her involvement?

*Possibly. We tend to list the more prominent or closer person first, which indicates that Priscilla was not timid.*

4. What traits of Priscilla should we emulate?

*She was hospitable, a teacher, knowledgeable, and brave to put her life in danger for Paul.*

## Reflection on Phoebe, Mary, Junia, Typhaena, Tryphosa, Persis, Rufus's mom, Julia, Nereus's sister

1. What are the main efforts Paul appreciates?

*Paul appreciates those that work for the church, work for the Lord, and have treated him as family. He also mentions those who worked in the early church. This would have been 30 years later, so those who have been Christians for decades through difficult times.*

2. What did Paul ask the group to do for Phoebe?

*Phoebe is the new Christian in town from Greece. The Roman church is asked to welcome Phoebe and to help her with her needs while she is in the area.*

### Reflection on Philip's daughters

1. What would it have been like to be a young girl who prophesied during this time?

*Women and young girls are dismissed in many cultures. It may have been frustrating to have the spirit of prophecy in a male dominated society. Or the early church may have been more receptive than later groups at encouraging women.*

### Reflection on Drusilla

1. What are some reasons Drusilla might have resisted becoming a Christian?

*Her royal and political position may have made it difficult to be humble. The life of a Christian may have meant losing power and privilege to Drusilla. Felix's reluctance may have influenced her negatively.*

### Reflection on Bernice

1. When you are called to act, but you choose not to act; what does that indicate?

*Jesus tells us that by our fruits we are known (Matthew 7:16-20). By Bernice's actions we know that she did not choose to follow Christ.*

### Reflections on Euodias and Syntyche

1. How does keeping our eyes on the bigger picture of the gospel help us handle personal disagreements?

*It shifts our focus from "my rights" to "our mission." It helps us see conflicts as temporary but the gospel as eternal.*

## Reflections on Apphia

1. How do you feel about having a church meet at your house every week?

*It could be a strain to have others, even wonderful people, over to the house every week. I might feel differently if I had servants, but it would still be challenging. I have a lot of respect for people that put that effort to support the church.*

## Reflections on Favorite Lady

1. What would be the strengths of the Favorite Lady?

*She was respected for truth, and the fruit seen in her children. She balanced love and obedience.*

2. What are areas the Favorite Lady should watch?

*John urges her to use discernment to guard against deceivers. She is expected to watch for problems.*

## Reflections on Jezebel

1. Why would a group filled with love, faith, service, and patience in Thyatira tolerate Jezebel and her followers?

Thinking of John's message in 2 John, where truth and love are matched. If love is given without truth, it becomes permissiveness. On the other hand, truth without love becomes legalistic. Thyatira may have focused on love, faith, service, patience, but was weak on following the truth.

2. What were the traits that the woman called 'Jezebel' shows?

*She was interested in the 'new religion' but didn't want to change from the other religions. She wanted the advantages of a Christian family and maintain a relationship with everyone else.*

Additional material at:
http://abiblestudy.com

www.ingramcontent.com/pod-product-compliance
Lightning Source LLC
LaVergne TN
LVHW020719110826
845149LV00012B/2337

* 9 7 9 8 9 9 4 9 2 8 9 0 5 *